The Baby Takers

Bret Oldham

Edited by **J. Smith**

Cover art by **Jeffrey Oldham**
Copyright © 2017 Jeffrey Oldham
www.oldhamart.com

Copyright © 2017 Bret Oldham

Published by
Halo House Publishing
Henderson, NV. U.S.A.

ISBN: 978-0-9891031-4-5

About The Author
Bret Oldham

Bret Oldham is a well-known alien abductee and paranormal investigator. He is known for his abduction experiences, his work with other abductees, and his EVP and Spirit Box work and research. Bret is the author of the acclaimed Amazon Best Seller, "Children Of The Greys," in which he details his lifelong alien abduction experiences. He has made several national television appearances in the United States, Canada, France and Bulgaria including shows on Bio, Discovery, CBC Canada, History Channel, TV7 Bulgaria, and RMC Decouverte in France. He has been featured on numerous Internet TV and radio shows and has been interviewed by various online magazines and newspapers. Bret has contributed chapters to several other books, including books by world renowned author Brad Steiger among others. He has also written articles for Alternate Perceptions and Mysterious Universe magazines. As a public speaker, he has been a featured guest speaker for Nevada MUFON, Tennessee MUFON, California MUFON, Para-Mania, Octagon Hall, Kentucky, Paranormal Study Center, Huntsville, Alabama, Fayetteville Art Center, Tennessee and various other ghost groups and UFO organizations.

Contact info – haloproductions@live.com

Table of Contents

Acknowledgements

Writing books on the subject of alien abductions is quite a daunting task within itself. Writing a book about your own alien abduction experiences is an even more daunting task and was one of the most difficult things I have ever done. So difficult in fact that for awhile I had decided I would never write another book. Yet I couldn't ignore the many requests from all over the world for me to continue my story. So, with the encouragement from those who found help and strength from my first book "Children Of The Greys" and of my family, friends and colleagues in the UFO field, I continue on my quest to reveal the truth with this book. I couldn't have done it without you all.

First and foremost, I would like to thank my family, especially my mother Loretta, Jeffrey, Haley, Annette and Dennis, for your unwavering love and support. I know that at times it hasn't been easy. It means more to me than mere words can express.

To my many friends for your continued support and belief in me and what I do, I give you my sincere gratitude. You've taught me the real meaning of true friendship. So many of you have not only helped spread the word about my story but you have defended me against those who feel threatened by it. You are appreciated and loved more than words can say.

To my brother Jeffrey Oldham, thank you for once again blessing me with your amazing artistic talent. Your vision and contributions have been invaluable and are much appreciated.

I owe a deep debt of gratitude to my talented editor J. Smith. You helped turn my story and message into a piece of work we can both be extremely proud of. Your hard work and dedication was awe inspiring. Thank you, thank you, thank you…

To all of you who reached out to me with your own story. I know just how difficult it was to get the courage to share such personal and traumatic experiences with a stranger. I hope that I've been able to help you find some peace and the strength to understand and deal with it. I applaud your courage and I am deeply touched that some of you have agreed to let me share your experiences here in this book. Your trust in me and willingness to help is greatly appreciated.

To Julie, your light pulled me out of the depths of darkness and showed me the way to finding myself again. Had it not been for you, this book would still be sitting unfinished. I cannot express enough my gratitude for your love, encouragement, inspiration and all you have done for me. Thank you for being the beautiful soul that you are.

Lastly, I would like to express my sincere and heartfelt gratitude to all of you in the media who have had me on your radio or television show, have interviewed me in your magazines or had me speak for your organization. It is because of you, the people who listen and watch your shows, and the people who buy the books that this message reaches the masses. It is of the utmost importance that the awareness of this subject is spread throughout the world. Thank you all for doing that and for giving me a medium to do the same.

Foreword

For millennia, our species has looked upon the vast sea of stars in the heavens and asked the same question. Are we alone? Answering this question is problematic for people. Some are afraid to entertain the idea that other intelligent beings exist in the universe. This fear prevents them from opening their mind to the possibilities. Others feel that human beings are the apex of creation. For them, it is impossible to believe that more intelligent beings exist in the universe. This idea of man's supremacy in the universe is common and widespread. For those holding this misconception, an awakening is in order.

Mainstream science accepts the possibility that life, in some form, exists on other planets in our galaxy. Planets capable of sustaining life are frequently being discovered. Many of those planets are located in the "Goldilocks Zone," also known as the "Habitable Zone." Recent polls indicate that a rather high percentage of the American public believe that there is life on other planets. This percentage, however, drops dramatically when the question is asked whether or not alien life forms have visited earth. The idea of an advanced species of aliens visiting or inhabiting our planet ignites a deep fear in many.

Fear and vulnerability create many questions. What would aliens want? What is their agenda? Would they be peaceful? Are they going to kill us and take over Earth? Will they turn us into a slave race? How will we defend ourselves against such an advanced species? Will they have the same God, or will we find out we have been wrong? Can we trust them? These are important questions, and the answers could dictate the future of our species. For most, it is easier to avoid these questions and simply carry on with their normal routines of daily life. They think "Maybe someday aliens will visit us, but not while I'm alive," or "It's something a future generation may have to deal with but not us."

While there are many people who choose to ignore these possibilities, there are literally hundreds of thousands of individuals around the world who know that aliens exist. Not only do they know that aliens exist, they also know that they are already here. They have seen them. They have been taken and subjected to a myriad of different experiments. These individuals are alien abductees, and there are many of them. Estimates range between several hundred thousand to four million people have had some kind of interaction with an alien species. Many of these encounters begin at an early age and are repeated many times throughout the life span.

While science tries its best to dismiss these alien abduction events as sleep paralysis or delusions, the evidence is mounting to the contrary. There is evidence that science cannot explain such as the presence of unexplainable scars, rashes, and unidentifiable objects in the body. Also, the phenomenon of missing pregnancies cannot be adequately explained. Abductions with multiple people reporting the same events have been documented. These alien abductions leave physical damage to the abductee but also severe mental trauma as well. This is especially true for those who have endured pervasive sexual procedures such as alien rape, forced intercourse with other humans, semen extraction and the removal of an unborn fetus from the body.

This book will focus on encounters with two alien species, the Greys and the Reptilians. The Greys are small, thin, gray skinned creatures with big heads and large black eyes. The Reptilians are large, bipedal, muscular lizard looking creatures. In my first book *Children of the Greys*, I went into extensive detail of my life long abduction experiences with the Greys. Since that book was published, I have been contacted by people all over the world who have shared their own personal alien abduction experiences with me. Many of these people had never told anyone about what they had experienced. Most were afraid of the consequences of revealing their secret. They remained silent and were left to deal with the trauma on their own. I understand that fear. I was once in that same position. I suffered in silence for over two decades before gathering the courage to write a book about my experiences.

The anonymous abductees whose stories are related in this book have much to share. Like me, they have been the victims of alien sexual experiments, alien rape, and fetus removal. They have seen the hybrid children that are the result of these sexual intrusions, and they, too, have had to deal with the psychological effects of these experiences. As for me, my story continues. My alien abductions have not stopped. This book is the voice for those too afraid to speak. This is their story. This is my story. We are not alone in the universe. We are not even alone on our own planet. The aliens are here. They have been here and are using us to create a new species. This is our alien hybrid reality...

Chapter 1

Propagation of a New Species

These days, when one hears the word "hybrid," the first thing that comes to mind is a hybrid car, one powered by both batteries and fuel. Not much thought is given to the concept in any other form. Yet, humans have also created hybrids in biological form by cross breeding plant and animal species. The *Merriam-Webster Dictionary* defines a hybrid in this way.

1:   *an offspring of two animals or plants of different races, breeds, varieties, species, or genera*

2:   *a person whose background is a blend of two diverse cultures or traditions*

3a: *something heterogeneous in origin or composition: composite-hybrids of complementary DNA and RNA strands*

3b: *something (as a power plant, vehicle, or electronic circuit) that has two different types of components performing essentially the same function.*

The Concise Encyclopedia defines it this way. *"Offspring of parents that differ in genetically determined traits. The parents may be of two different species, genera, or (rarely) families."*

One thing, however, not often discussed is the premise of an alien/human hybrid. Most of the general public believes that this is the stuff of sci-fi movies or, merely, the imagination of Hollywood writers. The reality of a hybrid species, being created by an alien race, is viewed as impossible. Furthermore, a large percentage of the population does not even believe that an extraterrestrial race has ever visited our planet or interacted with us in any capacity. These beliefs are stamped on our psyche at a young age and, as a result, are difficult to release even when presented with evidence.

In fact, there has been overwhelming evidence that alien races have been visiting our planet and interacting with us for millennia. Still, there are those who refuse to accept this evidence. They refute it, without even researching it. Cognitive dissonance is rampant, but the truth remains. The hit television series, "Ancient Aliens," produced by The History Channel, has been instrumental in bringing to light many new theories.

It has been suggested by some ancient astronaut theorists that modern day homo-sapiens were created by an alien race called the Anunnaki. This theory originated from stories found on ancient clay tablets. These Sumerian Tablets were discovered in 1850 by Austen Henry in Iraq, near the modern day city of Mosul. The tablets were written in cuneiform. Cuneiform is the oldest form of writing ever discovered. The Sumerians were a very advanced civilization, and no one knows where their knowledge originated. Many have speculated that it was given to them by the Anunnaki. In addition, the Sumerians were accomplished astronomers who developed their own star charts. Their unique language did not originate from any language on Earth. They also demonstrated advanced knowledge in the fields of education, law, architecture, agriculture and industry.

Zacharia Zitchin, a researcher and transcriber of the Sumerian Tablets, claimed that the Anunnaki were a race of extraterrestrials from a planet called Nibiru. According to Zitchin, the Anunnaki came to Earth in search of gold for their planet. Having the technology for genetic manipulation, the Anunnaki created modern day homo-sapiens by blending their own DNA with that of prehistoric man. The Anunnaki created this new race for the sole purpose of mining gold. If this theory turns out to be correct, then, in essence, we are all alien hybrids.

In recent years, Sumerian researcher, Michael Tellinger, discovered evidence in South Africa of gold mines and dwellings dating back 100,000 years. If accurate, this changes the timeline of the history of modern man. With thousands of tablets left to be transcribed, what further information will be gleaned? Will we learn more about the Anunnaki, and what role, if any, they played in our evolution and/ or creation? Will we discover that we are all alien hybrids? Does this explain the "missing link," and why as a species we suddenly gained intelligence that should have taken thousands of years? Perhaps, in time, we will know the answers to these questions.

The idea of an alien/human hybrid race is not new. In the Book of Genesis, the Bible speaks of "fallen angels" or Nephilim that came to Earth and mated with women. In essence, they created a hybrid race. Genesis 6:4 "There were giants in the earth in those days, and also after that, when the sons of God came in unto the daughters of men, and they bore children unto them, the same became mighty men which were of old, men of renown." The Anunnaki were described in the Sumerian Tablets as giant, muscular humanoids. Some believe that the Anunnaki and the Nephilim were one and the same. If the Anunnaki were responsible for creating modern day Homo sapiens, then why was it written in the Bible that God created man in his own image? Many questions have remained unanswered as to the origin of our species and our genetic code.

Our genetic code or DNA has been commonly recognized as the two strand double helix, but scientists have also identified an additional ten etheric strands of DNA. These extra strands of DNA have often been referred to as "junk DNA;" since, scientists have not been able to discern a probable use for it. If we were created by an alien race, perhaps, they had a purpose for these extra strands of DNA. Maybe, this DNA could be activated at some point to help mankind progress. Is it possible that one or more of these DNA strands have been activated in certain individuals in our history? Certainly, there have been extraordinary individuals who have changed history. Individuals like Leonardo Da Vinci and Nikola Tesla come to mind. These two, undoubtedly, used their gifts to help mankind progress.

When it comes to the creation story in the Bible, people have accepted this account without giving it a second thought. Ever since I was a kid in Sunday school, I have found the Book of Genesis to be confusing. I would ask questions to my teachers, but they would reply that we were not to question the word of God. That reply was not satisfactory then, and it is not today. I have heard many sermons in my life. No one has mentioned anything about giants, from heaven, mating with the women of Earth. Why would they avoid this story? Was it avoided because of its sexual nature? Did the church not want to deal with the idea of hybrids being created? If the Nephilim were not human and were "mating" with humans, then hybrids were being created.

History has been filled with accounts of both men and women having sex with some sort of supernatural entity. At times, this was consensual, and at other times, it was not. Even the story of Jesus began with his mother, Mary, being impregnated by a supernatural force, God. In times past, the credit was often given to demons for these otherworldly sexual trysts. If a person was a willing participant, then they were said to be possessed by a demon. If they were an unwilling participant, then they were said to have been attacked by a demon. These dogmatic religious beliefs were and still are the answer most often used. The demons, who perpetrated the sexual interludes, were given names. The *incubus* was a demon in a male form that pursued women in order to have sex and father a child. The female form of this demon was called a *succubus*. The hybrid offspring was called a *cambion*. Countries all over the world have some form of an incubus and succubus in their folklore; although, they may be called by different names. These mythical beings have been used, at times, to explain an unexpected pregnancy.

A succubus was said to take the form of a beautiful woman. This form would seduce men and then collect semen from them. The succubus, initially, appeared very beautiful and appealing but was revealed to have claw-like hands and serpentine tails. Many myths claimed that a man would awaken from a "dream" feeling exhausted. Anyone familiar with the alien abduction phenomenon could not deny the eerie similarities between these folklore stories and events told by alien abductees. Abductees have reported unexplained pregnancies, sperm extraction, exhaustion upon waking, and images of being seduced by a beautiful woman or handsome man. They have also reported hybrids being born from this union. Even the description of the succubus closely matched the descriptions of the Reptilian species. In times past, people had no way of knowing about events that happened to other people around the world. They also had no conception of aliens. Religious references were all they had to explain these unnatural encounters. Is it possible that the sexual relations attributed to demons were actually abduction events? There is no way to know with certainty, but the similarities seem to go beyond coincidence.

One of the first people to come forward and claim he had sexual intercourse with an alien was a young Brazilian farmer named Antonio Villas Boas. His case was the first reported UFO/alien abduction case in modern history. The event happened in 1957 when Antonio was twenty-three years old. On October 5, 1957, Antonio and his brother Jose witnessed an odd looking circular light from their bedroom window. This object appeared to move toward them. It then vanished instantly. Later that same month, Antonio and his brother saw a round UFO. It appeared to be firing beams of light in every direction. A few days later on October 16, Mr. Boas was, again, in the fields when he saw a red light begin to descend from the sky. As it got closer, he saw that it was an oval shaped metallic object. Three legs of a tripod came from its underside, and it quickly landed. A metallic ladder was lowered from the craft. Antonio was terrified. He started to flee, but his tractor engine died. Within moments, four beings were beside him. He described them as human looking and of normal height. They wore tight fitting gray uniforms and helmets.

Antonio was taken aboard the craft. His clothes were removed, and his body was wiped down with a colorless liquid. He was taken to a chamber containing a sofa. In this chamber, he was subjected to a colored gas that was emitted from the walls. The substance made him so nauseous that he vomited. Approximately an hour later, a nude white skinned female entered the chamber. Antonio reported that she had straight blond hair with red colored pubic hair. Her hair and lips were very thin. She had slanted blue eyes, and her high cheekbones made her face come to a point. Her body was the most beautiful he had ever seen. The young farmer claimed to be filled with uncontrollable sexual desire for the woman. He had sex with her twice during his time onboard the craft. As she left, the woman gestured to her stomach and then pointed to the sky. Mr. Boas claimed that the entire encounter lasted for approximately four hours. After the incident, Antonio suffered from various symptoms including sleeplessness, nervousness, and other strange physical symptoms. He sought medical help and was examined by Dr. Olavo T. Fontes. Dr. Fontes discovered that Mr. Boas had been exposed to high levels of radiation. As a result, he was experiencing radiation poisoning. Antonio Boas reported that these symptoms did not dissipate quickly but continued for a period of time after his encounter with the craft.

Based on Antonio's description of the extraterrestrial female, it appeared that she was an alien human hybrid. There were several similarities between the woman he had sexual intercourse with and the alien hybrid women I have seen and interacted with during my own abductions. Clearly, she was used to engage in sexual intercourse with him in order to become impregnated with sperm directly from a human source. It was also possible that, during this encounter, she was learning about human sexuality and its associated emotions. Antonio claimed that the alien woman made strange growling sounds as they were having sex. Were these sounds related to the expression of emotion during the sexual act? Most likely they were. It is my belief that alien hybrids are born with some human emotions. The Greys are keenly interested in emotional expression. As a result, Mr. Boas and his hybrid seductress were probably being observed and monitored during this sexual encounter. The Greys want to understand, not only, human emotional makeup but also the emotional makeup of the hybrid. The propagation of a new species is happening. It has been for a very long time.

Chapter 2

The Baby Takers Play God

Life is the most precious gift of all. This belief is a universal truth accepted by every culture around the world. The fear of losing life is our specie's greatest fear. No one knows how long he or she will get to enjoy this gift from God. This uncertainty makes it an even more valuable treasure. When a life is lost, it is a solemn occasion. We mourn, pray, and search for the strength to move on without that person. We feel a deep sense of loss. Loss and death are universal.

On the other end of the spectrum, we rejoice when a new life enters the world. For most expectant parents, the news of a baby coming is an exciting time. Modern medical equipment is able to show the growing fetus while it is still in the womb. Bonds are created, and parents love this baby even before the child is born. Most people know the sex of their unborn child and name it months before birth. The love and care for this unborn child begins immediately. Measures are taken to insure that nothing goes wrong during pregnancy. Then the child is born; proud parents, family members, and friends celebrate this new beginning, as the baby begins its own journey through life. This child has been given the greatest gift — life.

I am sure that many of you reading this book have experienced this joyous event on, at least, one occasion. Whether or not you are a parent, you, most likely, have felt love and happiness associated with a new birth. It is a beautiful thing. Unfortunately, for thousands of people, this joy is cut short. These are the women whose babies are taken months before they are born. They are taken by an alien species that most people do not believe exist. Because of the stigma placed on this subject by society, they are forced to live alone with a nightmare from which there is no escape. The trauma induced by such a horrific event cannot be emphasized enough. Imagine living a perfectly normal life. You have found out that you or your significant other is pregnant. You are happy about the prospect of being a parent. The new life is growing day by day, week by week. Ultrasounds are taken; you learn whether you are having a boy or girl. You discuss names and start preparing a baby room in your house. You announce the good news to your family and friends. All is going well. One night a few months into your pregnancy, however, you wake up to find yourself in a strange environment surrounded by hideous looking creatures. You discover that your clothes have been removed. You are on a table with your feet in stirrups. You are frightened beyond description. You try to gather yourself and rationalize what is happening. "This is all just a really bad dream," you tell yourself. You try to wake up, but soon realize that this is no dream. These "things" are taking your baby. You scream for help, but there is no one there to help you. You try to get away from them but you cannot move. Tears are flowing down your face as you beg them to stop, but they are not listening. You see them take your baby right before you black out.

This scenario or one very similar has played out time and time again for countless women all over the world. The medical community will not help even when they cannot explain it. No doctor will risk his career by claiming that an extra-terrestrial race removed a fetus, no matter how strange the circumstances There is no way to know just how many women have had this happen. Most, who do remember, keep quiet about the experience. That fact, in and of itself, makes it easier for the aliens to get away with taking a fetus. This is, probably, why they do not make an effort to suppress the memories of the event. Sometimes they return and take several fetuses from a woman over the course of her life. For some women, these intrusive incidents cause so much psychological damage that they give up the idea of giving birth to a child. They develop a fear of becoming pregnant. They fear, if they do become pregnant, the aliens will return and take the baby. I have always felt that this aspect of the alien abduction phenomenon is the most tragic. Oddly enough, it is also one of the least talked about and most overlooked areas pertaining to the alien abduction subject. To me, it is the main purpose of abduction for the Greys and the Reptilians.

In my first book, *Children Of The Greys*, I devoted a chapter to the time I experienced watching a fetus being taken from my girlfriend. That chapter and that incident struck a nerve with people all around the world. I decided to name this book after that particular chapter. After my book was published, I was invited to do numerous radio and television shows which gave me the opportunity to talk about some of the experiences that I wrote about in the book. The stories that garnered the most attention were the ones of sexual experiments and of fetus removal. I included the sexual experiences in my book because I wanted people to know what is really going on when one is abducted. Too many in the UFO community shy away from the sexual aspect of alien abductions. It is a taboo subject, but it is one of the most important things that should be discussed. It was embarrassing to include these experiences, but people need to understand that these alien encounters are much more complex than simply getting examined on a table and then released.

For those of you who are not familiar with my experience of witnessing a fetus being taken, I have included a long excerpt from my book containing the story. I feel it is important to include it here. The year was 1988 and the location was Las Vegas, Nevada. I was living with my girlfriend, Denise. I changed her name to Denise in the book to protect her identity given the nature of the subject matter. Denise had been on birth control pills but still got pregnant. I know that there is still a risk of pregnancy while using birth control pills, but that particular method of birth control is 91% effective. As a result, I have always felt that the Greys intervened to assure Denise got pregnant. Prior to this night, I had been having a series of abduction events. I had also begun to have mysterious nosebleeds again. Here is the excerpt from "Children Of The Greys."

'Because of the unusual circumstances of Denise getting pregnant while on birth control pills, her OB/GYN had requested her to make frequent visits with him until he was assured that everything was normal with her pregnancy. Denise was in good health, and soon the doctor was pleased with everything; both mother and child were doing well. We were both relieved that no problems had been found. Everything was going along with the pregnancy as it should. After a few more weeks, her gynecologist did an ultrasound. The ultrasound test also showed that the fetus was growing and progressing in a normal fashion. There was nothing in all of the exams and tests that indicated any sort of problem. Denise's doctor told her to keep doing what she was doing and that he wouldn't need to see her now for a few weeks. That was all good news!

Then I began to experience the recurring nose bleeds again. One morning I woke up to, again, find small droplets of blood on my pillow. I couldn't hide this from Denise, so I just explained to her that I was having some sinus problems and must be blowing my nose too hard. I'm not sure if she believed me or not. A week or so later, I woke up to find a substantial amount of blood stains littered about my pillow. The red blood drying against the pure white color of my pillow case created a very disturbing contrast. It was a symbolism of the truth, a glimpse of the consequences of a multi-dimensional reality crossing into my everyday reality. I stood and stared at it. I knew it was them. "Why are they coming for me so much?" I asked myself being careful not to show my dismay. "That can't be your sinus causing this Bret," Denise said. She continued, "You need to go to the doctor right away." "Calm down, calm down, I'm OK. Look, if it happens again I promise you that I will go to the doctor," I replied. "You promise?" She asked. "I promise. One more time and I'll go for sure" I said. That seemed to satisfy her for the time being. She seemed suspicious though, and I wondered if she knew that it was the Greys causing my nosebleeds from their procedures being done on me. If she did, she kept it to herself and never mentioned it. I was happy that she did, and then the unthinkable happened.

A few nights later, while Denise and I were both sleeping soundly, we were suddenly awakened by a loud bang in our bedroom. I quickly raised my head up to see what had caused the noise. As I did, I found that I was unable to move any other part of my body. There was a very bright light coming through the back window of the bedroom that lit the room up, and there they were. Standing in our bedroom were five extraterrestrial beings! They were small, thin, with large heads and dressed in matching dark tight uniforms. It was the Greys. I was horrified! Maybe it was from fear or maybe it was the Greys using their mind control, but I couldn't get any sound to come out of my mouth. I looked over at Denise and saw that she was also awake. She too must have been rendered immobile. She wasn't moving or speaking either. She was just lying there with her eyes wide open and a look of sheer terror on her face. The aliens were all standing still with no movement whatsoever. They stood there just staring at us with those big black eyes for what felt like an eternity. I don't think that they expected us to wake up when we did. From what I have observed during my abductions, I have concluded that everything the small Greys do is based purely on logic. When something illogical happens, it seems to confuse the small ones, and they become unsure of how to react.

I remember that two of the aliens were standing along the side of the bed where Denise was. There was a Grey at the foot of the bed in front of me and one standing beside it toward my side of the bed. One of the aliens had stayed in the back of the bedroom close to the area that opened up into the master closet and bath. I have no other memories of the aliens in our bedroom that night. It felt like everything went black about that time. The next thing I remember is opening my eyes and seeing a bright light. I was lying nude on some kind of hard surface table or bed that was just barely big enough to fit my body. I was completely surrounded by Greys. I didn't see any kind of medical equipment or exam devices around me this time; just Greys, all standing very close around me on all sides. I knew that this time something different was going on or maybe had already gone on without me remembering it. I was scared! There was no way to know for sure what was happening or what was about to happen. I knew that there must be a reason for them to be surrounding me like this. It was unusual for them to do that in this manner.

I was still unable to move any other part of my body, except my head. The Grey closest to my head leaned over me; his face was within a foot of my face. I didn't want to look at him. I wanted to close my eyes, so I didn't have to look at him; but I am unable. He was forcing me to look at him; I couldn't resist his command. I was forced to look into those deep, large black eyes of this insect looking creature. He began to communicate telepathically with me. They usually would try to calm me down when doing this, but this time they weren't. He told me that there was something he wanted me to see. The alien, next to him, must have known what he said to me. Right after he told me that there was something that he wanted me to see, the Grey standing on his right side next to him changed positions and moved around to the top of my head. I was getting very, very nervous. I hated it, the feeling of helplessness, the not knowing, and the apprehension of what was coming next. You never knew, with these heartless bastards, what they were going to do with you. I still don't!

When the Grey moved to the area at the top of my head, I turned my head to the right to see what else was in the room with me. When I did, I was shocked to see Denise lying on another platform table about fifteen feet away from me. She was also nude. There were several aliens around the platform she was on, but not by her left side. They had purposely left me an open view to her. They had her legs up and spread very much like a typical gynecological exam. I was furious at what was happening! Denise started to scream. I wanted to scream too, but I still couldn't. It was obvious that they let her cries be heard so that that I could hear them. "Please stop! Please don't hurt my baby," Denise begged the creatures. I couldn't bear to watch what they were doing to her, so I turned my head away. I could hear her crying and pleading with these extraterrestrial savages. I knew that I could do absolutely nothing to stop them; I felt helpless, useless, and weak. I felt them commanding me to watch what was happening with Denise. I fought their desire with all the will power I could muster and maybe for a few brief seconds it was working. Then the one, by the top of my head, placed his scrawny, clammy hand over the top of my forehead and turned my head back towards Denise. It was hopeless, and I knew it. I heard Denise again. "No! No! It's my baby! Please don't take my baby!" She begged. It was all more than I could handle. I began to play mind games with myself. I told myself that this wasn't real; that I was just having a very bad dream.

I tried to convince myself that all I needed to do was wake up, and everything would be alright, but this nightmare was real. I was living it and, deep down, I knew it was real. I had never before felt the kind of barbaric rage that I felt at that time. Suddenly I was able to speak, and I started screaming at these insidious pieces of shit with all my might. "You Bastards! I'm going to kill you! I promise I will kill all of you little mother fuckers!" I adamantly expressed. I meant every word of it too. My anger and rage was so intense. Had I been able, I know that I certainly would have carried out my promise and taken out as many of them as I possibly could have. Looking back now, I'm sure that they found it all very amusing. I was stupid. I had let them win. They wanted me to be upset. The Greys are intensely interested in our human emotions as I have stated in previous chapters of this book. Having experienced their mind experiments before, I soon came to my senses and realized what they were doing. I knew that they wanted me to observe the procedure they were doing to Denise so that they could monitor my emotional response to it. I also knew from past experiences that the only power I had in these kinds of situations was to do my best to show no emotion at all, and that is exactly what I did. I quit screaming and cursing at them. I quit looking at Denise and instead began to focus my attention on the lights of the equipment on the wall beside her. I did my best to block out what was happening to Denise. It wasn't easy. On the inside, I felt my heart was being ripped out; on the outside I remained stoic. I went into a zone and intensely concentrated on nothing but the lights of the equipment. It must have worked. That was the last thing that I remember from being on board their craft that night.

A beautiful, bright ray of sunlight was shooting through the bedroom curtains when I woke up the next morning filling the quiet room with an enhanced sense of calm. My body felt drained. I rose up and sat on the edge of the bed trying to clear my head. I noticed that I was not on my side of the bed. I leaned over and shook Denise. "Wake up," I told her. I continued, "Look where you are at. You're on my side of the bed, and I was on your side when I woke up." "Do you have any idea how we got switched?" I asked. Before she could answer me, I noticed that the old typewriter that had been sitting on a small table near the bed had been knocked over. Then I remembered the loud bang we had heard. "Look, the typewriter fell off the table. I wonder how that happened," I said to Denise. It was then that I started to remember the Greys being in our bedroom after we heard the typewriter crashing to the floor. It was the aliens that had accidentally knocked over the old typewriter. It was right by where one of them had been standing. I was about to ask Denise if she remembered anything about what had happened, but, before I could ask, Denise noticed blood on the bed. She got up and went straight to the bathroom. Then I heard her yell to me, "Oh my God! I'm bleeding! Call the doctor now!" I quickly jumped up and got dressed. Denise yelled again from the bathroom, "something's wrong. Something's wrong with the baby!" I called the doctor and explained what was going on. The nurse got the doctor on the phone, and he said for us to come in immediately. We rushed as quickly as we could to the doctor's office, which took about 15 or 20 minutes. Denise was examined, and an x-ray was taken. The doctor came back into our room with a distraught look on his face. "There is no baby," he bluntly said. "You had a miscarriage," he explained. He asked Denise if she saw any tissue come out of her, and she replied that she had not. There was only blood, no tissue at all. "You must be mistaken," the doctor said. He continued, "You were four months into the term of carrying this child. There would have been tissue." Denise assured him that there was no tissue that came out so he insisted that she be checked into the hospital for a procedure called a D&C to clean out her womb of the remaining fetus tissue.

I waited patiently in the hospital waiting room while Denise's procedure was being done. My head was spinning from all that had transpired in the last several hours. I kept remembering the horror of the night before. I couldn't shake it. It felt to me as if the aliens wanted us to remember it. I knew that they had taken the fetus. I saw them do it! Both my Mother and Denise's Mother had come to the hospital for support. Even though I appreciated them coming, I wasn't saying much to either of them. I was drained, and I knew that this event would be more emotional pain to carry with no way to release it. This time I wasn't alone. I blamed myself. If Denise had never met me, she would have never had to endure such an insufferable nightmare.

I looked up and saw the doctor coming towards me. As we all got up to greet him, he started shaking his head. I was worried. "Is Denise OK?" I asked. "She's fine, but this was the strangest thing I've ever seen. There was nothing in Denise's womb, no remaining tissue at all. Her womb was already cleaned. It was like the fetus just disappeared. I just saw her a few days ago and she had a perfectly normal pregnancy. Now it's as if she had never been pregnant at all, and we both know that certainly was not the case," the doctor replied. After the doctor walked away I looked at my Mother and said, "They took it." "Who took it?" She replied. "The Greys," I simply stated and said no more. I would later tell her what had happened, but right then I didn't have the strength to talk about it. I just didn't have it in me. I didn't even want to think about it.

Later that evening, Denise was released from the hospital. I felt numb. I didn't know whether to scream or cry. I was exhausted both physically and mentally. I had nothing left. I didn't know what to say, and I don't think that Denise did either. Maybe it was better that way. Maybe the silence somehow helped the healing process to begin. We both needed rest. The ride home from the hospital was somber and silent. I wasn't sure how much Denise remembered; I didn't want to bring it up and cause her more emotional trauma, so I kept quiet and waited. Several days would go by before Denise said anything, and we were able to talk about what had happened that night to us and to the baby. To my dismay, Denise also remembered it all. The Greys hadn't blocked or erased the memory of the event from either of us. There was nothing left to say or do now. Another life had been changed forever. The baby takers had come to visit.

In December 2013, I flew to Las Vegas, Nevada to film a segment for the show "Monsters and Mysteries in America," which aired on The Discovery Channel. During the interview with the producer, I was asked about the incident in which the fetus was taken. I related my account of the incident. They asked me if Denise would agree to tell her side of the story. I had not spoken with her in years. I had no idea what, if anything, she remembered about that night. I found her on Facebook and sent her a message. I asked her if she remembered the incident and if she was interested in discussing it on camera. A few days later she replied. She did remember, and she was still terrified that they would return and take her again. She agreed to do the filming. During the two day shoot my ex-wife, who I will refer to as Rena in this book to protect her identity, my mother, and brother were interviewed. On the second day, Denise was interviewed. I had no idea how much Denise remembered about that night. Out of curiosity, I asked the producer how the interview went. He slowly raised his head and looked me straight in the eyes. "She remembers almost everything exactly as you do." She backed up your story one hundred percent." The psychological impact of that horrendous night was severe. Even after all these years, neither of us had forgotten anything. I am sure we never will. Denise also appeared with me on an episode of "Ancient Aliens," in which we spoke again about that unforgettable event.

In March of 2017, I flew to Los Angeles to film for a new show which, as of this writing, has not been officially named. The show is being produced by Prometheus Productions, the company behind "Ancient Aliens." During the filming, I agreed to a hypnotic regression session which was done by Dr. Judy Bloom, a very qualified therapist. I was apprehensive about being regressed. Revisiting these events made me uneasy. I had no idea what to expect or what kind of memories, if any, would surface. I had come a long way in the healing process. I was in a good place, and I regularly counseled other Experiencers. I was concerned that I might suffer a major setback by submitting to the regression and reliving the trauma or, worse, uncover some event that had been suppressed. I could not ask any of the people I counseled to undergo regression if I was unwilling to do it myself. I had learned to face my fears, and I was determined to face this one too. I was about to face my personal demons again but this time with a room full of cameras, directors, producers, film crew and a therapist all focused on me. It was not the most optimal situation to undergo a regression session of this nature. I felt naked and vulnerable. I knew that a couple of million people might someday watch me go through this very personal journey down the rabbit hole. I also knew that I had to face the fear of what I might find head on, regardless of the circumstances. It was that important.

Before the filming began, I asked to speak privately with Dr.

Bloom. I wanted to feel comfortable with her. I also wanted to make sure that she would not ask any leading questions that could be misconstrued as guiding me in what to say. If anything came out, I wanted it to be straight from my subconscious. I wanted anyone that saw the session to know that too. She assured me that she would not ask or direct me in any manner. She asked me how deep I wanted to go during the hypnosis. I wanted to go as deep as I could. I told her that if I became agitated or afraid during the session to let it go; unless, she felt that my health was going to be jeopardized by the trauma of reliving the memory. She was surprised by my request but agreed to it. It was important to me to stand up to my fear no matter how emotional it was. After our brief conversation, I felt good about her. I trusted her. I was ready.

Two memories surfaced during the regression. One of them was a recent event that will be discussed in a subsequent chapter. The other was a memory of the night that the fetus was taken. It was a very emotional experience for me. I was not an outside observer, but I was experiencing it again just as it happened. The memory was very vivid. I got so lost in the moment that I completely forgot I was under hypnotic regression. The sounds, the colors, and the pain were all there in great detail. I became very upset during the regression just like when it happened in 1988. Once again, the myriad of emotions raced through my body each leaving their own indelible mark on my psyche. Most of the memory consisted of things that I already remembered; I was simply reliving them. As the event unfolded, I became more and more emotional. The horror of this event was almost unbearable, but Dr. Bloom honored my request and let the memories continue to unfold.

I got to a point where my initial memories ended. I was now venturing into unknown territory. The Tall Grey removed the fetus. He immediately turned and left through an entryway behind him. Denise stopped screaming. She was just sobbing as she stared at the ceiling. A small Grey changed positions and went to do something between her legs. I could not see what he was doing. I called out to Denise, but she ignored me. It seemed that she had gone into shock. I frantically tried to get her attention. "I'm sorry. I'm sorry." I repeatedly told her. "It's my fault. I'm so sorry. It's my fault." I continued in my vain attempt to apologize. She never once acknowledged my presence. After Dr. Bloom brought me out, I felt numb. The room was silent. I had been lying down, and I slowly raised myself. Dr. Bloom asked me how I felt. I felt a bit woozy. The emotional impact of reliving this insidious event had drained me. I was told later that tears were rolling down my face. I did not feel embarrassed that a room full of people had just witnessed a grown man cry. Nor did I care that a large television audience would, most likely, do the same. It was real, raw emotions. I was not weak for crying; I was strong. After a few minutes, I felt better. It was then that I realized my guilt had been lifted. I had always felt that what happened was my fault. By going through it again, I saw that there was absolutely nothing I could have done to stop it. I had tried, but I could not move. The Greys had immobilized me. I also let go of the notion that Denise was just with the wrong guy, but that was not my fault either. I never asked to be taken. I never wanted it. How could any of it be my fault? I had carried a heavy burden for a long time, and now it was gone. The regression was traumatic, but facing those fears again was a very enlightening experience. I had come a long way in the healing process. That day I made more progress.

People have a difficult time accepting the reality of these types of abductions. It is one thing to hear about someone's claim of being taken by aliens, given a quick examination, and then returned home. It is something quite different when an unborn baby is taken. For most, this is too much to comprehend. Fear takes over. The very thought of such a thing ignites a fear that we, as a society, are ill equipped to handle. There is nothing that we are taught that prepares us for such a reality. We are raised believing that we are the supreme beings of the universe. We are the ones in control. We believe that we are micro versions of the God we worship. We cannot fathom the notion than an advanced race would use our DNA to create a hybrid race. The idea of women as human incubators is also very disturbing. It is much easier for the public to dismiss this phenomenon as a delusion of unstable individuals rather than live with the reality of the truth.

The social stigma is so great that the majority of abductees who experience such a horrific event never tell anyone. Although the aliens are able to suppress the memories of abduction, they seem to leave the memory of abductions in which a fetus is taken. Perhaps, it is done to monitor, through implants, the emotional and psychological impact the event has had on the individual. Perhaps, they want the abductee to remember it so when they are introduced to a hybrid child they will believe that this is their child. The aliens want the abductee to believe that they are indeed one of the parents. The Greys, in particular, want us to interact with the hybrid children. They insist that you do. Even though they can force humans to interact, through mind control, they do not resort to that method. It seems important to them that a natural bond is formed. The subsequent interaction between human and hybrid child is what they monitor. This is exactly what happened to me a few years after I witnessed the fetus being taken. The female hybrid child on the cover of "Children Of The Greys" is a depiction of the child they presented to me. The encounter with the small alien hybrid child that night had a profound impact on me. I never forgot her. I knew that if I ever got the courage to write a book about my story, I would put her on the cover. I wanted the world to know what she looked like. I wanted the world to know she was real and out there somewhere.

I cannot say, with certainty, that the hybrid child was mine. I have no way of knowing if she was the fetus taken that night from Denise. They had taken sperm from me numerous times, so it was also possible that she was created from that. Maybe she shared none of my DNA. I tried to resist having anything to do with the small hybrid girl. I tried not to feel anything for her, but I did. Even though I was only with her for a short time, there was a bond formed. I will never forget the softness in her eyes as she looked at me. I would have thought that she would have been afraid of me, but she was not afraid. I must have looked strange to her. I was so much bigger, but none of that mattered. It was like she knew too. Many years have passed since I met her. She would be an adult now, perhaps having children of her own. I never got to see her again. I have often wondered if I will ever get to see her again before I die. I wonder where she is now and what her life is like. I have wondered if she was integrated into our society. Maybe I have passed her on the street and never knew it. Since she was so young at the time, I wonder if she remembers me. I am angry at the Greys for their complete lack of empathy. I am angry at them for never letting me see her again. Do they not understand the psychological effects of these separations? Do they just not care?

It is difficult to live your life as an alien abductee. I cannot express how difficult it is. My heart goes out to anyone who has had to endure these experiences. It can be too much of a burden for some to bear. Recently, I heard of two abductees who committed suicide. The psychological damage of their abduction experiences was too great. They could no longer cope with the resulting anxiety stemming from their abductions. The physical scars from the experiments eventually heal. I have unexplainable scars on several areas of my body. Yet, I have no memory of how they got there. I think this is our subconscious protecting us. Whatever happened to me was so terrifying that my subconscious mind keeps me from remembering it. It is the body's own way of self preservation. I have had several doctors examine my scars over the years, and none have been able to explain how I got them.

In April of 2015, I went for my yearly physical. This time, I brought Rena as a witness. I had a new female physician who had never seen the mysterious scars on my body. I opened up my medical gown and showed her the scars across my spine. As I expected, she was perplexed. She suggested a special blood test that might help solve this riddle. The blood test came back negative just as I knew it would. She told me that she had consulted with another doctor in the clinic, but neither had any explanation as to how I got the mysterious scars.

There have been skeptics who have said that an advanced alien species would not leave scars since their technology is so advanced. Of course, there is that possibility. Perhaps, they leave scars on purpose. I cannot adequately express the complexity of what is happening with alien abductions. It goes way beyond the physical nature of it. They are monitoring our minds on a continual basis. They leave us signs all the time. Leaving the body with scars is a part of a master plan. It is another emotion to monitor. I also see no reason for them to be concerned about removing them. In the case of the Greys, as I have previously stated, they lack empathy. So why should they care if they bring us back with scars, unless it is done purposefully for their own benefit?

I am not the only one with unexplainable scars. Thousands of abductees have come back with unexplainable scars on their bodies. Other physical evidence is left as well. The physical things like scars, rashes, and nosebleeds are easier to cope with than the mental scars. This is where the lasting damage is done. This is what pushes someone over the edge to take his own life in order to escape the never ending horror of these abduction events. One of the most difficult things to cope with is the forced sexual procedures. Women and men (yes men) are being raped by these beings. Some abductees report forced sexual encounters by the aliens themselves, especially within the Reptilian species. There are many reports of alien hybrids raping both male and female humans. Mind control is used with the unwilling male human in order to facilitate this process. Most human male encounters are with female alien hybrids. I wrote about my experience with a female hybrid Grey in my first book. Sometimes humans are forced, using mind control, to have sex with other humans. I believe this is done to serve two purposes. One is to create a fetus with the genetic makeup that they prefer. Secondly, the Greys and, perhaps, other alien races seek to understand humans in order to understand the hybrids they are creating.

Finally, one of the most traumatic things experienced by an alien abductee is having your baby taken by these beings from another world. I know from my own experience and the experiences of others how profound the effects are. The sense of loss, the emptiness, the feeling of helplessness, and the anger all remain. A wound is inflicted that time never completely heals. How could an advanced alien race be capable of such an intrusive, despicable act? I came to grips with that question a long time ago. They do it because they have to. I do not adhere to the premise that they are, necessarily, evil, but the act itself could be considered evil. When it happens, it changes how you view not only our planet but our species. You realize just how fragile and vulnerable we are. You understand the need humans have to believe in a God who can protect them. Accepting that a superior extraterrestrial race exists and is using us to create a hybrid race is very difficult to do but necessary. The Baby Takers are here. They have been here, and they will continue to play God until their agenda is completed. What that means for our own feeble race remains to be seen.

Chapter 3

Unstoppable

I always hoped that someday the Greys would be done with me. I wondered what it would be like to live the rest of my life like a normal person; I cherished that thought. Eventually, I learned this was a false hope. That dream would never happen. With much reservation, I came to accept my fate. I knew, if I let it, my life would be ruined. I was determined to not let that happen. I have worked hard to overcome the psychological and physical obstacles that these alien abductions have brought into my life. I have learned to empower myself here and now, since I have no power during these abduction events. I have no say in whether or not I am taken; I cannot control what procedures and experiments are performed. Eventually, I took a Zen approach. I took a step back, looked at my life, and found positives in these alien encounters. Identifying the positive has helped me cope over the years. I accepted the fact that the aliens are unstoppable, so I let go. I told myself that I, too, would be unstoppable.

By letting go of the anger and bitterness, I was able to take back my life. Occasionally those old feelings come back to haunt me. Sometimes, the demon of depression will, once again, try to coax me into believing in him. Sometimes, I think about what I have endured, and I begin to feel sorry for myself. It took me two years to write my first book about my experiences because I had to fight off these inner demons. In the end, I won. I did not let the Greys steal my life from me. I turned the tables and looked at everything in a different light. I have been healthy my entire life which I mostly attribute to them.

They have hurt me, but they have also healed me. My view of our world changed has changed for the better because of what has happened to me. My religious beliefs also changed, and this freed me from the confines of fear based dogma. I found strength I never knew I had. The realization that I made it through decades of these experiences gave me the assurance that I could make it through most anything. Fear was erased from my life. When you are no longer a slave to fear, you find out what freedom truly is. After all the things I have seen and been subjected to, what could I possibly face that would scare me?

One of the most valued things I have taken from my experiences is the ability to communicate with the spirit world. Had I not had my body's vibrational frequency changed by the dimensional portals, then I might not have the powerful chi or energy that I have now. As a result, I have been able to help people in our plane of existence and many confused souls on the other side as well. My friend, Brent Raynes has conducted numerous ghost investigations with me. He noticed that I was receiving a large amount of spirit communication. He told me about a theory in which it is believed that someone with increased energy could "seed" others around him, and they too would have their psychic abilities enhanced. I have seen some impressive energy develop with me and others. Maybe, there was something to "energy seeding;" it certainly was an intriguing theory. My energy increased as a direct result of my abduction experiences, and this is one of the positives that I have taken from my experiences. I felt it for many years, but I resisted it because of the negative stigma associated with any kind of psychic ability. That has changed. I have learned to embrace it. I am grateful that I have been able to help people find peace in this world and in the next.

Since I went public with my story, I have been asked many great questions. One question often asked is "Are you still being taken?" The answer to that question is a resounding, "yes." Unfortunately, the abductions have not stopped, but the event parameters of the encounters have changed. The experiences have shifted to include new locations and new species. I have written previously about the correlation between alien abduction and increased paranormal activity. After the publication of my story, the paranormal activity around me increased substantially. I have had a lifetime of ghostly encounters, but, for some reason, a wide array of paranormal events began soon after *Children of the Greys* was published. It has been speculated by some that the Greys were upset with me for revealing my story to the world. I do not believe this. If anything, I was doing the Greys and the governments of the world a favor by bringing more awareness to the reality of alien abduction.

Having reached a world-wide audience, I do believe I caught their attention. The Greys have the ability to control the thoughts of abductees through the use of implants. This is achieved through synthetic telepathy which enables them to maintain a direct conversation with your thoughts. Since the implants measure the sensory information of the abductee, the Greys are able to view what the abductee is experiencing through his senses. As a result, they were, most certainly, aware of what I was saying and doing during this time; they began monitoring me more and began to increase the number of times I was taken which, most likely, further enhanced my energy levels. As my energy increased, the paranormal activity surrounding me did as well. I will go into more details about the use of implants in a later chapter.

One of the things I began to notice was the movement of objects around the house. These objects, at times, even disappeared; some unseen force was playing tricks and, perhaps, purposely trying to cause confusion. This kind of poltergeist activity had happened to me in the past but not to this level. Spoons began to disappear at an alarming rate and were never found. I started to notice household items in unusual places far from where they belonged. One day, I was home alone eating lunch in the kitchen. I heard a loud thud that came from the spare bedroom. My first thought was that the mirror had fallen again. No matter how well I secured the mirror in that room, it would not stay on the wall. When I walked into the bedroom, I found the mirror on the floor again. I picked it up, leaned it against the wall, and left the room; I went back to finish my lunch.

A few minutes later, I heard what sounded like a clanging noise coming from the same room. I got up to see if I could determine the source of the noise. As I entered the room, I immediately noticed that several framed photos had fallen over on the table. I set them upright and placed them back in their proper place. A few minutes later, it happened again. This trend continued with other pictures around the house. I took it in stride since these kinds of things had happened to me in the past. It was and is a part of my life. I wanted to help the restless spirit so I conducted a brief EVP (electric voice phenomena) session using my digital recorder. I recorded a male voice, but all he did was acknowledge his presence. If he would not let me know what he needed, I could not help him. I politely asked him to leave my stuff alone, but he did not listen. Over the course of the next few weeks, the high strangeness continued.

One day, as I was leaving the house, the ghost made his presence known again. I had a habit of putting my three dogs in the kitchen before leaving the house. I installed a gate across the entryway of the kitchen to contain them in that room. My dogs always seemed to know when I was about to leave. On this day, I gathered up my things, put on my jacket, picked up my car keys, and called out to the dogs that I was going "bye-bye." This was a word that they recognized and understood. The dogs all ran into the kitchen knowing that I was about to shut the gate. I walked across the den to close the door to the gate. As I passed by the French doors, I heard the click of the locked dead bolt open. Upon hearing the deadbolt, I immediately stopped; I was within a few feet of the French doors. The door had been securely locked, but I could see that it no longer was. Something had turned the deadbolt to unlock the door. As I stood there looking at the door, I saw the doorknob slowly begin to turn. Then the door swung open, all by itself. It seemed that my dogs were not the only ones who knew that I was about to leave. After that incident, I was a bit hesitant to leave; I wondered what the ghost might be planning. "What kind of surprises would I come home to?" I silently asked myself. I spoke out loud and politely to the unseen house guest. "Thank you for opening the door for me; that was very thoughtful of you." Perhaps, they were just trying to be helpful because when I returned home, everything was in order.

It was during this time, spring and summer of 2013, that I began to hear the "hum" again. There had been times in the past, when I occasionally would hear a low frequency pulsating hum that others did not hear. Thank God, it was not constant. It would come and go but was disturbing, none the less. Because of the frequency of this sound, I decided to reach out to several friends of mine who were also alien abductees. Strangely enough, several of them reported to me that they, too, had been hearing the same type of sound. Hearing this unexplainable hum was not new to me. It had happened many times. I began to feel a sense of dread come over me. The hum, in the past, had been a precursor to an abduction event. This time would be no exception.

My psychic awareness began to increase to new heights. I began to have more difficulty going to sleep at night. Sleeping had always been a problem for me. Decades of being taken had left me with sleep disturbances. In addition, there was a steady stream of spirits seeking me out, especially as I tried to sleep. Between the two, I rarely got a good night's rest, but this was my reality. During this time period, as I lay in bed trying to fall asleep, I would hear entities speaking. This, in and of itself, was not unusual for me, but this time it was different. There were lots of voices. They were talking in full voice but not to me, to each other. It sounded like a cocktail party. I could hear them speaking to each other, but I could not make out what they were saying. Because I was hearing the hum on a regular basis, I was worried that an abduction event was imminent. Not only was I dealing with the fear of abduction, but I was also dealing with these voices every night.

Had the Greys returned me without closing the portal properly? I pondered the possibility and feared the repercussions. It seemed to me that I was hearing a parallel dimension. Maybe, it was a party or some kind of gathering in another dimension. Whatever it was, they seemed to be completely oblivious to me. This was not the usual spirit communication I had experienced in the past. The beings, behind these voices, were not seeking help. Why could I hear them? I mentioned this to my friend, Sandy Nichols, on the phone one afternoon. Sandy, also an alien abductee, has had paranormal events happen to him on a regular basis. To my surprise, he told me that he had also been hearing voices that seemed to be coming from what he thought was a parallel dimension. Was there a connection? I wondered. It seemed strange that both of us were having the same strange phenomenon happen. We, not only, lived in the same area but were also abductees. I did not feel good about it. The increased paranormal activity, the dimensional voices, and the pulsating hum all happened soon after my book was published. Was it simply a coincidence? I did not believe in coincidence. Everything happened for a reason. Unfortunately I believed that all this increase in paranormal activity meant that "they" were returning. I soon learned that my intuition was correct.

I did not remember being taken to the "intake room," during this abduction. The intake room was a small room where I was always taken first. From there, I would be escorted to other areas depending on what kind of experiments or procedures were performed. My first conscious memory of this experience was being escorted by two small Greys. I was dressed in a white, tight-fitting outfit made of soft, stretchable material. They had never dressed me in white. Most of the time, they did not dress me at all. The two Greys were walking slowly behind me. I did not know where I was supposed to go, but I sensed that I was to keep walking until ordered to stop. Although I felt very coherent, I was already under their mind control. It bothered me that the aliens were walking several feet behind me. This was not their usual behavior. My thoughts began to race. "Are they afraid of me now?" I wondered. I made another quick glance behind me to see if there were more of them, but all I saw was a long, dark corridor. I briefly considered making a run for it, but where would I run? I did not recognize this location. They would have stopped me anyway. Something, however, did not feel right about this corridor. The lighting was dim and was not the type I remembered. It looked like ours. The floor was a dull gray with a slight sheen to it. Even the walls looked different. I began to suspect that I was in a facility made by humans.

My anxiety soared as different scenarios began to play out in my mind. I had gone too far; I thought to myself. I convinced myself that they were upset that I had written and published a book about them. I remained silent like I had done on so many occasions. I felt like a death row prisoner taking those last mournful strides before his execution. "This is why they took me somewhere different. "They are not going to bring me back this time," I told myself. I wanted to ask them where we were going, but I knew the small Greys would not answer me. They would just give me one of their programmed replies such as they would not hurt me, or I was going to be alright. I knew these beings. I knew that, soon enough, I would find out what was waiting for me at the end of the corridor, even if that meant death.

We reached our destination, and I was even more perplexed. We entered into a chamber where a small triangular shaped craft was docked. The back of the craft opened up, and I was telepathically told to enter. The first thing I noticed was that the cockpit was in the nose of the small craft. Two human looking men were sitting in the cockpit. One of them turned around as I entered the craft. He looked at me but did not speak. These men, wearing black body suits, looked exactly like men I had seen previously. Perhaps, they were clones created by the aliens to be used as workers. I was stopped beside a series of clear cylindrical tubes. There were three of these on each side of the craft. I was shocked when the small Greys instructed me to get in one of the tubes. Being claustrophobic, the last thing I wanted to do was get inside a tube. My heart was racing, but I was forced to obey. I reluctantly slid into the clear tube and lay down. This felt like a terrible nightmare, but I was not asleep. I was sure this was the beginning of my demise. Sadness and despair overwhelmed me. I was upset that I would never get to say good-bye to the ones I loved. "How could these heartless creatures treat me this way after all I had given them?"

Little did I know at the time, but the real nightmare had just begun. I was lying still, inside the tube, when I heard more footsteps. I was not paralyzed, and, yet, I made no attempt to move. I turned my head to see who was responsible for the footsteps. Humans were coming into the room. In a strange way, I felt a certain amount of comfort at seeing other human beings. If they were going to kill me, at least, I would not die alone. Maybe, this was another one of their human sex experiments. This had been the case, in the past, when brought in close proximity to other human beings. For a few brief minutes, I felt some relief. They began to place the other humans in the remaining tubes on each side of the craft. My tube was on top of the other two on one side of the craft. No one was speaking. Suddenly, they started to seal the tubes; I started to panic. I tried to get out, but it was too late. They closed my tube. In an instant, I felt the craft move. As it took off, I could see a large window above my tube. As I lay, helpless and trapped, all I could see was darkness coming through the window. Seconds later, the darkness was replaced by white waves of water. I felt like I was suffocating and I screamed, "Let me out! Please let me out!" My frantic pleas for mercy fell on deaf ears. No mercy was given.

The anxiety from this horrible experience exploded into a panic attack, and I passed out. When I regained consciousness, I was still in the tube but no longer in the small craft. I had been placed in a large room that resembled a warehouse. The feelings I experienced, at that moment, were indescribable. It felt like I had been underwater, so I assumed I had been taken to an underwater base. I had no idea where I was or why I was there. I had no idea what was going to happen to me. I tried to control my breathing and remain as calm as possible. This would be the ultimate test. My will to live was strong. I would do whatever it took to survive this ordeal. I wanted to go home again. If I was going to die, then I was not going to die without a fight. I looked for a way to escape. As I did, I noticed the tube containers were filled with people. Some were conscious, and others were not. I could see fear in the eyes of these poor, unfortunate captives. The tubes were at least thirty feet off the ground. I could see rows of tubes below me and across from me. All the captives were wearing the same white clothing. Whatever was happening, it appeared to be very organized. It was eerily quiet. The silence was deafening. I could only hear the sound of my breathing. I wanted out!

I, then, noticed a mechanical device that looked like an automated forklift system. It was attached to guide rails that ran along the wall. The device was silver or chrome in color. It came from the entry and treaded along the wall. It, then, turned and slowly moved along the large shelving, where the tubes were placed. The shelving was open with only rails holding the tubes. The apparatus moved to an area below me, and I could no longer see what was happening. In less than a minute, I saw it again. It had attached to the shelf and removed a tube. I could see someone in the tube, but they were not conscious. I could not believe what was happening. I felt like nothing more than a product in a factory. This process repeated several times, and, eventually, it latched onto my tube and pulled me out of the room.

I could not see anything after I was removed from the large ware-house. The lights in the subsequent room were blinding. The tube I was in, and everything around me, was engulfed in a sea of bright, white light. I tried to open my eyes fully but to no avail. The last thing I remembered seeing was a figure approaching my container. Then, everything went black. My next memory was being escorted, once again, by a Grey. This time there was only one Grey with me, a Tall Grey. We were in a large structure with a half dome shaped ceiling. It looked like a giant hall. We walked a few feet and came to the end. As we approached the end, I could see that the wall at the end looked like glass. The top of it was divided into two windows with each window in the shape of a half moon. I could clearly see the outside environ-ment through the upper windows. Whatever this structure was, it was under a large body of water. All the pieces of the puzzle were coming together. The small triangular craft had taken me to an underwater base somewhere on Earth.

I had no idea why, but I felt calm. Maybe, I was simply relieved to be out of the tube. Maybe, it was the presence of the Tall Grey. I had been with him many times. He was a leader and, at times, had answered some of my questions. He had tried to befriend me, from the beginning, at age five. There were others like him, but this one had always interacted with me. Maybe, I felt a sense of peace, simply, from still being alive. I had worked myself into a mental frenzy during this event. I was not home yet, but I had the sense that I was going to make it through this ordeal and return home. The Tall Grey stopped about 150 feet from the back wall. I was in awe of what I was witnessing. The room was impeccably clean. Rows of sophisticated equipment with hundreds of multi-colored lights lined the walls on each side. Up to this point, there had been no communication between me and the Tall Grey. I gathered my courage and asked him, "Why am I here?" He replied telepathically, "I wanted you to see this. It is important that you do." He then raised his long spindly arm and pointed towards the middle of the room where an octagon shaped object rose from the middle of the floor. It looked to be about seven feet tall and had an approximate six foot circumference. All of a sudden, the object lit up except for the top part, which looked like a lid. The light source was moving with great force. To me, it looked like some type of power source. It was more than, merely, light. I marveled at what I was seeing even though I had no idea what it was. I looked over at the Tall Grey. As I did, he lowered his head in a gesture for me to once again look at the octagon shaped object. When I did, a symbol appeared in the light source. The symbol was large and remained constant. I recognized it. It was the Japanese symbol for chi (energy).

That was all I remembered of the event. I do not know how I was returned, nor do I know the full extent of what was done to me. It began as a harrowing experience and ended with peace. I do not understand the relevance of being shown the symbol. What was the Tall Grey conveying to me? Was he showing me an energy source that is used in the underwater base? Was he simply reiterating to me that everything is energy, or did it all have something to do with the reason I and the other humans were taken to this place? Maybe someday, I will remember more and find my answer. Two things I do know. They are unstoppable, and they will come again. For now, however, I choose to relish my life, the people I love, and home.

Chapter 4

The Message

It has been decades since I was first taken by the alien visitors. I have had many alien abduction encounters since that first night when it all began in rural southern Illinois. I have witnessed and experienced things that no human being should, and I have shared many of these alien encounters publicly. After many years of experiences, I eventually learned about the hybrid program being implemented by the Grey aliens. The Tall Grey, who had befriended me so long ago, would sometimes answer my questions regarding the reasons for my abductions. Once, he showed me a room full of fetuses floating in, what looked like, artificial wombs. I did not agree with what was being done, but I began to understand it. I sensed a certain degree of desperation among the Greys. The hybrid program was a means to an end. To what end, I did not know.

I have interacted with some of the hybrids that the Greys have created including the female child that was said to be mine. I have seen what appeared to be human clones; each one looked like an exact copy of the others. They were white males with an average build and short dark hair. Unlike the aliens, they communicated by speaking audibly just as we do. I have also interacted with adult female hybrids that clearly had DNA from both humans and Greys. Once I was shown a small, grotesque baby that appeared to be the results of a failed experiment. It was a shock when I was first introduced to these new species. I had seen and experienced many things. I had been shown fetuses in artificial wombs. I had had my sperm taken numerous times.

I had been subjected to sexual experiments. I had watched a fetus being taken from my girlfriend, but seeing the results of their hybridization program was unbelievable. It was frightening to see its extent. They have been very successful at achieving their goal of creating a hybrid species. Their deception, intelligence, and technology have allowed them to have their way with our species.

I have never been so naive to believe that the Greys are the only alien race visiting or inhabiting our planet. I am sure there are others. If other races are here, what is their agenda? Just as the Greys have an agenda, so do the others. Some say that the Greys' plan for mankind is a sinister one. Others say that alien species are here to help mankind. I would like to believe that a highly advanced species would be here to help us advance, but, maybe, that is wishful thinking. We may never know the truth. They hide in plain sight. They know how easy it is to manipulate the truth. They know the belief systems of our planet, and they use them against us. It is also suspected that some work in conjunction with various governments or black op factions.

The Greys are one of the alien species who possibly work with a faction of the American government/military. This is not a big secret. Most people, who believe in UFOs, suspect this is the case. These various extraterrestrial species may have some kind of secret agreement with governments around the world. Do they have agreements between themselves and other alien races? Given that all have to possess the technology to be here, it is only natural to assume that they must be aware of the other's presence. Are the Greys the only ones with a hybridization program? Are other alien races also creating a hybrid race and if so, why? Are any other aliens participating in the Greys' hybrid program? These questions have gnawed at me for years; I had no idea that some of them would be answered during the summer of 2013.

The answers came quite unexpectedly during an abduction event in 2013. One summer night, I was taken. I was dressed in a tight dark body suit which was unusual; they usually left me nude. My first recollection of the event was walking with two small Greys down a narrow hallway. I knew that I was in a craft. The shiny floor and the rounded slopes of the walls looked familiar. The Greys were not communicating directly with me, but I knew that they wanted me to walk forward. They were not holding on to me as they usually did. Something was not right. It all seemed so casual. I had been through this same ordeal countless times, and there was always complete organization. Everything was done in an orderly fashion. This time, however, was different. It was too relaxed and too casual. It was not the way they normally operated. Strangely enough, because of their behavior, I, too, felt much less anxious than normal.

We reached a curve in the hall, and my alien company stopped. I did not know what else to do, so I waited for them to initiate some kind of communication with further directions. One of them looked down the hallway. As he did, I heard the word "continue" in my head. I hesitated for a moment before proceeding. I did not trust them. I looked back, and they were no longer walking with me. "This must be another one of their mind fucks," I told myself. I thought, "Fine. Go ahead and try it, but I'm not playing along." I hoped they were monitoring my thoughts. Maybe, they would realize that I was not going to participate and would cancel the experiment. I had been through this so many times. I was not the weak minded victim that I used to be, and they knew it.

As I rounded the short curve in the hall, the walls and the ceiling suddenly disappeared. I looked down and could still see the same shiny silver floor, but that was the only thing that remained the same. There was no ceiling. All I could see above and below me was blue sky and layers of white wispy clouds. I was immediately disoriented. I felt dizzy, and I stumbled. My disorientation seemed to be a result of the sudden change in depth and height perception. I regained my balance and continued to proceed forward. Slowly I advanced. I took great care to stay in the middle of the floor. I tried not to look down. It occurred to me that I was giving them exactly what they wanted by showing all of the emotions associated with my predicament. I reminded myself that none of it was real. I began to walk faster as I lost the fear of falling. I looked ahead rather than at my feet. As I continued, I saw what looked like a small wooden house approximately fifty feet ahead of me. It looked like something from the 1950's. The narrow surface that I was walking on led right to the entrance of the structure. There was a door frame but no door, just an open entryway.

"What now?" I asked myself. I had no choice but to enter the building. As I stepped through the doorway, the lighting changed. It resembled the lighting of earth. The building had only one room with an old wooden floor. There was a man sitting in a wooden chair in the middle of the room. He appeared to be human. I quickly noticed that he was not dressed like me. He had on regular clothing, baggy pants and a dark button-up shirt. He even had on worn leather shoes. He immediately spoke to me. He was speaking out loud and in English, but I knew this trick. They once had created a scenario using memories of my departed stepfather, so I had seen this technique. It had all seemed real then too. "Hurry and come in," the stranger demanded. I refused to reply to the man in the chair. Instead I shouted out to my captors, "You are not fooling me. "I know none of this is real!" Again the man frantically addressed me, "Hurry, they are coming!" I was caught off guard by his last statement. "Who is coming?" I asked. He replied," You know; you know who they are."

I could sense the fear in his voice as he replied. I then heard another voice in the room. It was the sound of a woman sobbing. I looked to my left and saw a dark haired middle aged woman. She was huddled down in a fetal position at the far end of some kind of large white vat. I was so focused on seeing another human sitting in the stark empty room that I had not taken the time to fully look at the rest of my surroundings. The only two objects in the room were the wooden chair and this large vat. The vat was empty. It was about six feet wide and ten feet long. The depth was about three feet. The woman sitting in the vat was clearly upset. Again the man spoke up, "They're coming; they're coming!" This time the nervousness in his voice was even more elevated. He suddenly rose up from the chair and hurriedly joined the woman at the far corner of vat. He continued to beg me to get away from the doorway and join them in the vat. It was very obvious that their fear was unfounded. There was no one here but us, and, at that point, I did not believe that any of this was real. I was not feeling fear, and I damn sure was not going to let it overtake me and give the Greys the reaction they wanted. I knew that I was being observed and monitored. As soon as they got what they wanted, this would all instantly vanish. It had always worked like that in the past. Why should this time be any different? The only thing that bothered me was that they had let this scenario go on for such a long time. I decided to play along with them. I obliged the wishes of the two human looking beings. I walked a few steps further into the middle of the room. I, then, heard footsteps approaching the building. "They're here!" The man in the vat exclaimed. He continued, "Get in now, please!" The woman in the vat began to sob uncontrollably. As the footsteps drew closer, I walked over and climbed into the vat. I sat down at the opposite end, away from the others.

What happened next came as quite a shock to me. A creature, the likes of which, I had never seen before stepped through the doorway. Real or not, it scared me. I knew that the Greys could pull memories from the subconscious mind and use them to create these holographic worlds. It was all done to illicit certain emotional reactions. Knowing this, I was confused. They could not have pulled this creature from my subconscious mind because I had never seen a creature like this and would, therefore, have no memory of one. My anxiety level started to escalate. I began to entertain the thought that this might be real.

The creature took large steps as he walked to the middle of the room. He slowly turned around and faced the vat. I was very afraid of this thing. I got up from where I was sitting but stayed in a crouched position. I began moving like a soldier trying to avoid enemy fire. As quickly as I could, I made my way to the other end of the vat and sat down by the man and woman. They were squeezed together in the corner. Both of them were sitting with their knees to their chins and hands wrapped tightly around their legs. I did not want to look at the alien, but I could not help myself. He stood there for what seemed like an eternity. We were both staring at each other. I could not believe what I was seeing. I was, both, in awe of the specimen and afraid of him. I knew, from his appearance, that he could kill me in an instant if he desired.

He was clearly a hybrid, but it was a mix that I did not think was possible. He looked like a cross between a human, Grey, and Reptilian. His skin was pasty white. His head was shaped like a Grey's but smaller. His eyes were the same bluish grey color of the female hybrid that I had seen but more slanted. He had no hair anywhere on his body. He was approximately six feet tall and very muscular. His arms were long like a Grey but muscular like an athlete. His four fingers were also long like a Grey but thicker. He had a small nose and mouth. It looked like he had small ears as well. The skin on his chest was a brighter color of white. The texture of his skin was also different on his chest. It appeared rippled like some kind of chest plate. He was wearing no clothing of any kind. He was completely nude. As if his appearance was not shocking enough, I noticed something else peculiar about him. The creature was male because he had a penis. This was the first time I had seen a male alien nude. I had speculated that male Greys might not have a penis or any type of anatomical part that served a reproductive purpose. Perhaps, it too had atrophied like the rest of their body. This was not the case with the hybrid standing before me. His penis looked very much like a human male uncircumcised penis. It also had testicles similar to a human male. One striking difference was that the testicles on this alien hybrid were overly large and disproportionate to the size of its penis. Like the rest of its body, there was no hair in the pelvic region.

The alien hybrid walked to the opposite end of the vat and stepped over the edge to get in. The other two people in the vat were crying and screaming. I felt the adrenalin rushing through my veins like hot lava. I did not know whether to fight this thing or try to escape. My inner sense told me that I could do neither, so I just sat there in silence awaiting my fate. It came towards me. I felt so helpless and small, as I huddled below the forbidding figure. I gathered what little courage I had left and slowly lifted my head. As I did, the creature leaned over me. I saw him raise his arm. His hand approached my head. I did not move; I was frozen with fear. I saw one of his fingers as it came toward my forehead. The tip of his finger was flat and not rounded like a human finger. He touched me between my eyes at the spot of the third eye. I instantly blacked out and remember nothing more of the incident.

The next morning I felt physically and mentally drained. I remembered the entire incident. I was upset with myself for showing emotion. I felt weak for being afraid of the new hybrid. They had beaten me again at this mental chess game. Checkmate Greys. I tried not to be so hard on myself, but I could not help it. I had reached the point where I faced fear. I had refused to let fear dictate my life, but I had succumbed to fear of this new creature. I realized, once again, that the Greys were clearly in control. What puzzled me the most was wondering which parts of the experience were real and which parts were created by the Greys? The old house was not a part of their craft, so, obviously, that part was not real. The old wooden chair did not belong either, but the large white vat could have been real. I have never figured out if the other two humans were actually flesh and blood people or not. I thought, at first, that they were there as a means to enhance my fear. Perhaps, they had seen the alien hybrid, and that is why they were so afraid. After much thought, I believe that the Greys showed me the hybrid to let me know that they were not working alone or that they were using other species beyond humans in their hybrid program. Another strange aspect of the encounter was the touch of the alien hybrid. He touched me in the area of my pineal gland. I related this story to a friend of mine who made an astute observation. She asked me if I had noticed an increase in my psychic abilities since that incident. I had never considered that correlation, but, upon reflection, I realized that there might be something to that idea. I had noticed a definite increase, especially in regards to spirit communication and precognitive abilities. Had this creature activated my pineal gland? It appeared that this was quite possible.

Also, the alien hybrid was nude for a reason. The Greys knew that it would shock me, and they wanted to observe my reaction. They also wanted me to think about the implications so they let me remember the experience. Maybe, they knew that I would tell as many people as possible like I am doing in this book. They wanted me to see the penis and testicles of the hybrid. It seemed to be their way of showing off. "Look what we can do now. We can reproduce." It was also an ominous message that the Reptilians were involved in some capacity. Were they somehow involved with me too? This was the message I took from this experience and the one that worried me the most. It was difficult enough to deal with the Greys, the human clones, and the

Grey/Human hybrids. Now a new element had been added to an already complex puzzle. I had received and understood their message, but there were more messages waiting on the horizon.

I have awakened many mornings with unexplainable scratches, bruises, welts, and rashes. Strange anomalies, appearing on my body, were not new. Most of them, I attributed to the experiments done to me by the unwanted visitors. During 2013, I experienced two very unusual incidents. The first unexplainable event happened in broad daylight. I walked to the kitchen sink to rinse out some plastic water bottles. I rinsed out one of the water bottles and set it down to dry. All of a sudden, I felt a sharp stinging sensation on the top of my right hand. I looked down at my hand and saw blood pouring from my hand. At first, I thought I must have cut myself, but I had not touched any sharp objects.

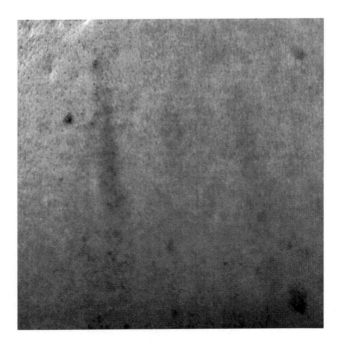

Large scratch marks down my shoulder blade
I once woke up with.

The blood was gushing out of my hand, so I grabbed a dish towel to hold over my hand. After compressing the area for a few minutes, I lifted the towel. The bleeding had subsided. I rinsed off the excess blood and dried the area with the dish towel. After I did, I could see two small, evenly spaced puncture marks. I was baffled as to what caused the puncture marks to appear on my hand. To me, it looked and felt more like an injection than a cut. I ruled out a bug bite since the area never swelled, and I found no trace of a bug. Interestingly enough, a bruise formed under the two puncture marks, and it took a long time to heal. I made a joke to Rena that I was experiencing stigmata but deep down it freaked me out. I felt as though I had been the victim of a covert operation. It was like some unseen entity, perhaps cloaked, had snuck up on me and injected something right into my vein! I had seen the Greys use dimensional portals, so I knew they could come and go in an instant. If I had been injected, then why? I cannot say what caused the puncture marks on my hand that afternoon. To this day, I am still searching for a plausible explanation.

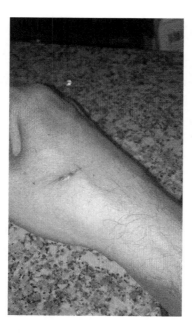

The puncture marks on my hand

Not long after the incident with my hand, I had another extremely upsetting physical anomaly occur. I woke up one morning feeling groggy. I sat on the side of the bed for a few seconds trying to gather the energy to get up and get dressed. I immediately felt an intense pain in my mouth. My tongue was so sore that I could barely move it. "Damn! I've bitten my tongue in my sleep," I thought. I quickly walked to the bathroom mirror to see how bad it was. I opened my mouth and stuck out my tongue to get a closer look at the damage. My eyes widened with disbelief. It looked like part of the front left side of my tongue had been removed! A section about 5/8 of an inch long and 3/8 of an inch wide was gone. It looked like a precise cut, almost in a half moon shape. It was swollen and still slightly bleeding. There was no way that I could have bitten off a chunk of my tongue in my sleep without waking up writhing in pain.

I have no memories of how it happened. I have assumed that, if done by aliens, it was so traumatic that my subconscious blocked it from my memory. My experience with the Grey/Reptilian/Human hybrid led me to believe that I was not only a part of the Greys' experiments but quite possibly the Reptilians' also. This, in and of itself, caused me deep concern. If that thought was not bad enough, I now had a deep gash on my tongue that took over two weeks to heal. My speech was impaired, and it was difficult to eat. Even now, I have noticed my enunciation is affected with certain words. I wish I had the answers as to what happened to me. I do not want to believe that it was abduction related, but I cannot find any other rational explanation. If it was them, what was their purpose? Worse yet, what would they do next? I could only wait and see; I prayed my conclusions were wrong.

I have said many times, both in print and on various radio shows, that the only constant fear I have is the fear that other family members will be taken. I know that the Greys, in particular, have an affinity for staying with a family line due to certain genetics. I shudder at the thought of anyone having to endure what I have at the hands of these beings. During the course of our marriage, Rena had never had anything unexplainable appear on her body except a small bump behind her left ear. We suspected this might have been an implant. It was in the same location as a bump I have. It made sense that they would implant an abductee's partner in order to monitor the thought patterns and emotional reactions to the abductee. Even though Rena had had some unusual dreams, she had no real memories of ever being taken.

The morning of October 21th, 2013 the paradigm shifted when Rena woke up with weird scratch marks on her neck. Not only did she have unexplainable scratches, so did I. We had not been up long that morning when I noticed the scratches on her collarbone. There was one on each side of her clavicle bone. Both marks were almost the same length. I pointed them out to her and asked if she remembered itching during the night. She stated that she had not been itching and had no idea how she had gotten the scratches. I found it strange that there was one on each side of her collarbone in roughly the same location. It looked like something with very large hands and long fingernails or claws had grabbed her around the neck. I was puzzled by it. After a brief discussion about it, we chose to go about our day and not give it further thought.

Rena went to the kitchen to make breakfast, and I jumped in the shower. I had no sooner gotten under the stream of hot water when I felt a burning sensation on my leg. I looked down and saw a five inch cut running down my leg. I quickly finished my shower and toweled off. I called out to Rena with a sense of urgency in my voice. This was not a slight scratch. This was a cut. Rena heard my voice and hurried to the bathroom. "What happened?" She asked, thinking that I had somehow injured myself in the shower. I shook my head and answered, "I don't know. It was there when I got in the shower." I continued, "It had to have been there when I woke up. I just didn't notice it until the water hit the cut." Whatever had happened to us that night, it now had our full attention. We knew the chances were slim that both of us would wake up on the same morning with scratches on our bodies.

Neither of us could remember anything from the previous night. We could not even remember what we had dreamed about that night. It was a blank slate for both of us. I did not want to entertain the thought that both of us had been taken, but I could not get it out of my mind. I was not sure how Rena would react to the idea that she, too, may have been abducted this time. There was a chance that we had both been attacked by some negative entity. We did consider that possibility. The problem with that conclusion was that we would have felt the pain immediately and woken up. My apprehension grew as I gathered the courage to speak to her about my suspicion. I took a deep breath and told her that I was worried that the Reptilians might have taken us. I had told her previously about my encounter with the new hybrid creature and how that possibly indicated involvement by the Reptilians.

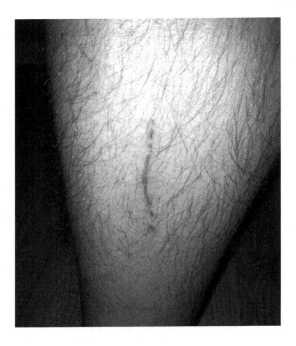

Cut on my leg

For a few brief seconds an eerie silence filled the air. She finally spoke, "but I don't remember anything." "Wouldn't one of us remember something like that?" she asked. "Not necessarily," I answered. I continued, "Maybe whatever happened was too much for us to handle. Maybe it's one of those times when our subconscious won't let us remember." I explained to her how the marks on her collarbone matched up with a large clawed hand wrapping around her neck. Perhaps, they were leading her somewhere and inadvertently cut her. Maybe she had struggled to get away, and they gripped her more tightly which left the scratch marks. We talked about what might have caused the cut on my leg. If we had been taken by the Reptilians this time, then possibly I was resisting. Could they have grabbed my leg with their claw-like fingers and caused the cut? We were both deeply concerned, but at this point, it was all conjecture. All we knew, for sure, was that we both had awakened with unusual scratches and cuts for which there was no explanation. A month later, a profound event occurred.

The first glimpse of sunrise came streaming through our bedroom window that chilly November morning. The rays of the sun slowly seeped through the small crevices of the blinds and curtains reminding us that it was time to awaken. It was one of those mornings when you felt so snug beneath the safe confines of your warm, comfortable bed that you did not want to move, but that was only a wishful fantasy on that particular day. We had much to do. We peeled away the soft warm covers and rose to start the day. As Rena made her way to the bathroom, I decided to go ahead and make the bed since we had a busy day ahead of us.

I was standing on my side of the bed as I began to straighten the sheets. I grabbed a hold of the sheet to pull it up and that was when I first saw it. It was blood. I spoke out loud, "What the Hell!" There on the bed, between our pillows, was a large area of what looked like dried blood. I quickly called out to Rena in the bathroom, "are you bleeding?" "What?" She asked, sounding confused by my question. "There's blood on the bed. Lots of it," I yelled back through the closed bathroom door. She quickly opened the bathroom door. "Oh my God," she cried out and gazed at the large blood stain on our sheet. "Where did it come from?" She asked. "I have no idea. We need to check ourselves," I replied. Rena assured me that she had not been cut. I was not bleeding either. It had not been long since we had risen one morning to discover scratches on us, so we checked each other again for any new cuts or scratches. We found nothing. Neither of us had suffered a nose bleed during the night, and there was no blood on the pillows. Wherever the blood had come from, it did not appear to be from us.

We looked closer at the area of blood. It was then that I noticed that the bloodstain looked like a four fingered hand. It was a bloody hand print. The print was made by a left hand, and it looked as though the print was made while leaning over Rena. We were both speechless. It reminded me of the handprints young children make while finger painting, but this was not art work. They were not using paint. The shock of finding this repulsive remnant left us shaken. My head was spinning as I frantically attempted to piece together this puzzle. Based on the size and shape of the hand print, I did not believe that it was left by the Greys. The length of the fingers was too short, and the width of the fingers was too wide. It also appeared to have long fingernails or claws. I was now convinced that I was no longer being taken only by the Greys. At the very least, the Grey/human/Reptilian hybrids were involved or, possibly, the Reptilians themselves. It was all making sense to me now.

I was also deeply concerned that Rena was now being taken too. Had my worst fear been realized? If so, I knew that I was totally helpless to stop it or prevent it from happening again. I was sick about it. I felt violated. My mind was racing with questions. One thing was certain. The messages from the alien visitors had not stopped. They were clearly letting me know who had the power. They wanted to reiterate to me that they would take whoever they wanted regardless of how I felt about it. That was why the hand was positioned over Rena. They were doing their best to keep us locked in a prison of fear, and, at the time, it was working. We did not know where the blood originated. I shuddered at the thought of some creature with a blood soaked hand leaning over Rena. What kind of insidious beings would do such a thing? What had they done to us? No wonder neither of us could remember anything regarding the horrors we possibly endured or witnessed that night. It would be too much for any person to take. The point of no return was close, and I knew it. I had grown used to these events. I had worked hard to overcome the mental damage left by them, but this was all new to Rena. I was worried that some memory of the event would seep through and reveal the awful truth to her. I was not sure either one of us could handle it.

I took photos of the blood stain to document it. We then removed the sheet and wrapped it up to preserve it in the hopes of someday having it analyzed. There were more questions than answers. Was it human blood, animal blood or possibly even alien blood? If it was human blood, then whose blood was it? Neither of us was bleeding that morning, and if we had been bleeding, blood would have been smeared everywhere. This hand print contained a substantial amount of blood, and it was between our pillows. The location of the blood stain would indicate a head wound or nosebleed. There was no evidence, on either of us, of that. Aside from that, the blood stain was in the shape of a hand print. Eventually, I arrived at a conclusion that I didn't want to believe. The Greys were not only abducting me, but now some form of a Reptilian was too. They were also showing me that they could take Rena, and they wanted to make damn sure we both knew it!

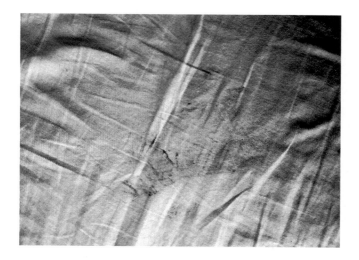

Hand print on sheet

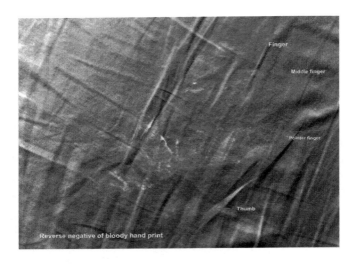

Reverse negative of hand print on sheet

Rena knew that I was afraid that someday she would be taken. We had talked about it many times. My gut instinct was that she had already been taken by the Greys. I had never seen her during any of my experiences, but I felt that they had taken her. Since neither of us had any memories of her ever being abducted, it was easier to just pretend it never happened. She had told me of recurring dreams of babies, but neither of us felt compelled to explore them further. Dreaming about babies does not, necessarily, indicate one has had an alien abduction incident. Rena did not exhibit any of the typical characteristics of someone who is an Experiencer. That was a good thing. After all, it was difficult enough to deal with my own abductions let alone your spouse's too. I have lived with the effects of being an Experiencer for over fifty years. These abduction experiences, along with the paranormal activity that usually surrounded them, have made my life anything but normal. If you lived with me, your life would not be normal. That was the cold, hard truth. Before this incident, we had no hard evidence that Rena had been taken. We left it at that and hoped that it would never happen. The incident with the bloody hand print, however, brought to life the very real possibility of it happening.

There is no way to prepare for an alien abduction. The experiences vary so much from the length and frequency of the event to the experiments performed. The only thing an abductee can do is accept that you have no control over any of it. Rena had learned all of this from me, but I still felt compelled to discuss this further with her. She understood and was not worried. If she had been taken, she did not feel that it would affect her everyday life since she had no memories of it. I knew, for at least the foreseeable future, she was right. Someday things might change if any memories surfaced. These unconscious memories are like a time bomb waiting to go off. No one knows how long the fuse is. For some abductees, they die before the fuse ever reaches the bomb. For others, memories explode into their consciousness with a force so great that it sends them toward a new reality – the reality of truth. How you handle that truth will determine whether you win or they do.

I was worried about what was next. The alien intruders had visited us two times within a matter of a few weeks. I wondered how soon until they returned. I wanted to know who was coming into our home. Were they working with the Greys, for the Greys, or completely alone with their own agenda? I decided to set up a motion sensor IR camera in the master bedroom in the hopes that I could catch whoever it was on film. I knew it was a long shot. These were extremely intelligent beings. I was sure that they would sense the equipment psychically or that their equipment would detect and disable it. I also considered that the use of dimensional portals would prevent them being caught on film. A few minutes to them might be a millisecond in our timeline; they would be in and gone before any of our equipment ever sensed them. Never the less, it was worth a try. I set up the camera in a position that captured the entire bed in the frame. I also decided to use a digital recorder. If I could not capture them on film, then perhaps I could record the sounds of an event.

Every night I would engage the camera and the digital recorder. The following day, I would review the video taken during the night. I caught the same thing every night which was one of us getting up to go to the bathroom. The motion sensor on the camera was so sensitive that it would trigger the video to record when one of us merely rolled over in bed. After several nights of this, I realized that my idea was not going to work. I needed a surveillance system that recorded constantly all night long, and I did not have one. I gave up on that idea altogether. After all, I had no idea when or if the aliens would return. I did not have the time to spend every evening going over the video. I did use the digital recorder for several hours each night. I spent several hours every day listening to the playback. This was easier to do than watching video because I would put on headphones and listen to it while driving or doing other chores around the house. Sometimes I would load the files into my audio software that I use to analyze EVPs. (Electronic Voice Phenomena)

I was catching some ghost EVPs, but that did not alarm me since I knew that our house had frequent spirit visitations. I could catch EVPs from the spirits day or night. I knew from all the paranormal activity happening in our house that ghosts were present on a constant basis. I was listening for a different kind of otherworldly presence. One evening, I loaded the files from the digital recorder into my audio software and started my routine of listening for anything that stood out from the norm. I had just begun to listen to the file when I caught a female spirit talking about us as we went to sleep. It was evident that she was observing us getting into bed and preparing to go to sleep. She heard us say goodnight and commented that she liked that. It felt like an invasion of privacy. Spirits were watching even as we slept. Picturing spirits surrounding your bed was not a very comforting thought. That, however, was often my reality.

A couple of hours into the recording, I began to hear a flurry of spirit communication. It was not just the woman I had heard speaking earlier. This time, there were several ghosts talking. They were commenting about the crystals on the nightstand. They were making other observations about us, as we slept. "He knows," a male voice told the other spirits. I did not know if he was talking about me or another spirit. I was fascinated but also a bit freaked out by what I was hearing. I had never left a recorder running during the night. It made me wonder how often this kind of thing happened. I then heard a weird sound coming through the speakers. It sounded like some kind of machinery. I rewound the file to isolate and loop the sound. I listened again and again but could not figure out what could have produced this odd metallic noise. I had never heard anything like it. I decided to continue with the audio review and listen for more possible clues. All of a sudden, I heard an emotional response from a male spirit. "Oh my God Oh my God." He sounded frightened. I was stunned by what I was hearing. I had captured thousands of EVPs, and it was rare to hear a ghost that sounded frightened. Sometimes, they were afraid of us, but, even then, it would not be caught on your recorder. They would simply retreat to another part of the location to be left alone.

In this situation, the ghosts in our bedroom had not seemed frightened. Since we were sleeping at the time, we were not even aware of their presence. They were there of their own accord and had no reason to be scared of us. Who or what had elicited that kind of a response from the male spirit? That single EVP created an avalanche of questions. As a paranormal researcher, I use inductive reasoning to sort out the facts of a case and come to a conclusion. I did not have enough facts in this case. I needed answers and had only questions. Can the dead see aliens too? Does the alien portal pass through the spirit world dimension? Does the spirit world dimension occupy and overlap with our own dimension? Since the spirits can see us in our dimension, then, perhaps, they can also see an alien who enters it. I had recorded EVPs stating they had seen me on their side. I had not died or had an NDE (near death experience). Perhaps, the spirits had witnessed me being taken through their dimension by my alien abductors. This revelation by the spirits might give us further insight into how aliens use the dimensional portals to take humans and how the dimensions are layered around these portals.

Did the male ghost witness alien creatures taking me, and did this cause his unusual remark? There are those who will say that the male spirit witnessed a demon. I have been told by certain religious people that aliens are demons. I disagree. In all my decades of paranormal investigating, I have never come in contact with anything I considered demonic. I have encountered negative entities or earthbound spirits that were angry or confused about certain aspects of their life. It was this intense negative emotion that kept them attached or bound to earth.

I have recorded countless EVPs of spirits proclaiming to be

demonic, but I have found this to be a futile attempt by the spirits to scare the living. I have never seen any credible evidence that proved the existence of demons. Movies and television shows have used this idea to scare people and make money. Even cases of so-called demonic possession seem to only occur among people with strong religious beliefs. I have never met a demon possessed atheist. Have you? I do not believe the male spirit saw a demon that night. What could have elicited such a profound reaction from a nonliving entity? Given the remarkable incidents of the previous few weeks, it was obvious to me. The aliens had returned. The message was clear.

Chapter 5

The Laughing Children

It takes courage to go public with a story like mine. I am not saying that to pat myself on the back. It took me more than twenty years to get the courage to go public with my alien experiences, and it has not been an easy ride. There have been many times since my first book was published that I have regretted ever writing and revealing what happened to me. I have been called names. I have had people lie to me and about me. I have met people who were afraid to be around me. I completely understand why so many "experiencers / abductees" keep quiet. Thankfully, I have also had tremendous support from both the general public and my friends and family. I do not think I would be able to continue without it.

I continue because my journey is not complete. I still feel it is of the utmost importance that the public know just how widespread the alien abduction phenomenon is. It is more difficult to come forward with one's story than most people realize. Fear of ridicule and embarrassment keeps the majority of Experiencers from going public. Many will not even tell trusted friends and family their secret. The social stigma, associated with this phenomenon, silences most abductees better than the memory suppression techniques of the aliens. Still, there are those who heard my story and felt compelled to reach out to me. Many of them, simply, wanted to be heard, and others found answers from my story which validated their own experiences.

Not long after *Children Of The Greys* was published, I was contacted by a woman whose story intrigued me. When I decided to write this book, I wrote and asked her if I could include some of her experiences. She graciously gave me permission to do so with the agreement that her identity not be revealed. For the purpose of telling her story, I will call her Mary. In hearing Mary's story, I learned that she has had encounters with two alien species, the Greys and the Reptilians. This, in and of itself, is more common than one would think. There are multitudes of abduction cases where the abductees report witnessing Greys and Reptilians working in conjunction with each other. Debates still go on as to which species is in charge and why. I am not sure that really matters. It could be that neither is in charge. It is possible that each species has its own agenda. It is also entirely possible that they share the same agenda. I do not think anyone truly knows. We only know that some Experiencers have encounters with one or the other, and some have encounters with both species. Thus is the complexity of the alien abduction phenomenon.

Mary was 23 years old when she remembers having her first incident with an extraterrestrial. It was the Greys. Personally, I suspect that she was taken at a much younger age than that and simply does not remember it. I was also in my early twenties when I first began to remember my abductions by the Greys; although, they began when I was five. The memory suppression induced by these creatures is highly effective. Some Experiencers remember a little. Some, like me, remember much more. Some remember nothing and go through life completely oblivious to the reality that they were taken. Those are the lucky ones.

I have spoken about the connection between alien abduction and increased paranormal activity for a while now. Not only did it happen to me, but I have found it is prevalent with other abductees. The high rate of paranormal activity is especially prominent in individuals who have been taken repeatedly from a young age. Those whose experiences started at an early age, I refer to as "lifers." The prison connotation is not to be overlooked. Abductees are prisoners, not in the sense of being placed behind bars in a cell. Still, they are prisoners. Prisoners with no pardons, no release date, and no benefit for time served. We are lifers.

Even though Mary believed that her first event with the Greys did not happen until she was twenty three, she was experiencing unexplained paranormal phenomena long before that. Mary mentioned to me that when she was a child she would often see what she described as "plasma balls," brightly glowing energy orbs floating through her house. She remembered times when the lights would go off and on for no reason. She also reported various other ghostly occurrences. I explained to Mary that these kinds of supernatural events were quite common among those of us, who have been taken by aliens. I went on to tell her how common it is for a multiple Experiencer to come back with some sort of increased psychic awareness. I hesitate to call it a "gift" since there are many fake psychics in the world who claim to have a "gift." This increased psychic awareness seems to vary from person to person, but it is always there in some form with abductees. Mary was no different in that regard.

I was shocked and saddened as I listened to Mary recall a horrifying event that happened to her as a child. "I was raised Roman Catholic. You can imagine how well paranormal stuff went over. When I was in the 4th grade, I hugged my mother at school and suddenly blurted out that I was going to have a baby brother. My mother pulled back and proclaimed, 'You're full of demons; you're full of demons!' She said that in front of the whole classroom. I found out later that my mother was indeed pregnant. She told me that there was no way that I could have known that she was pregnant since she had just told my father over the phone. Aside from my father, a nun, and a priest in our church, no one knew. I was really young and I was like, 'what have I done?' Soon after that, my mother had an exorcism performed on me and sent me to a Catholic school." Mary had to pay the consequences for using her psychic abilities; even though, she had no way of understanding them at that young age.

Mary also suffered from reoccurring nightmares as a child. She would often wake up in the middle of the night screaming from these terrifying dreams. Many times, she would see what looked like giant talons in her bedroom window. Given her later experiences with the Reptilians, I had to ponder the possibility that these events were, possibly, early Reptilian visits. Mary's parents dismissed her nightmares, her reports of bright objects floating in her room, and the talons in the windows as childhood imagination. Unfortunately, this is often the case when children report any kind of supernatural event to their parents. Children do, sometimes, imagine things. Often, there are perfectly rational explanations. There are cases, however, where there is no rational explanation, but phenomena are still attributed to a child's vivid imagination. Even if one was to ascertain that the paranormal activity witnessed by Mary as a child was simply conjured up by her young mind, it still does not explain her psychic ability. She knew that her mother was pregnant and also the gender of the unborn child. Given her memories of alien abduction and contact that later surfaced, I would lean heavily on the conclusion that Mary had been taken at a much younger age than she remembered. The psychic abilities, nightmares, and paranormal events were a direct result of those abductions.

Eventually Mary's memories of her experiences became too much to bear. Like so many others who have endured these alien abductions alone, the cracks in her armor began to widen. Like me, Mary began to suffer severe anxiety and panic attacks. She began to question her sanity, so she sought help. She sought answers. "I went to a mental hospital." Mary revealed. "I walked in and said I think I'm either schizophrenic or require some kind of medication. I approached it this way. If I was delusional or I had some kind of mental illness, then I needed to seek help and get on the proper medication. I knew that I couldn't keep going on like that." I empathized with Mary as I listened to her relate her experiences. I, too, had once sought professional help, as do many other abductees. When memories begin to surface, it is natural to be in denial. Then, the anger arrives, and a myriad of other emotions may appear. I understand why Mary went to a mental hospital for help. It is the most logical answer. "That's it! I'm going crazy!" You try and convince yourself. It is when you come to the realization that you are indeed sane, that your life crashes down on you like an avalanche. I cannot emphasize enough how difficult it is to psychologically handle these events, especially when you are doing it alone. Mary went through three days of testing at the mental health facility and was diagnosed with Post Traumatic Stress Disorder with associated panic and anxiety attacks. She was released and told that they could help her with symptoms of PTSD but could do no more.

Mary's first memory of abduction was possibly a botched abduction attempt by her extraterrestrial visitors. "I woke up in the middle of the night with my face pressed up against a popcorn ceiling. I remember thinking how could this be happening to me. I remember the pressure of the sharp, prickly things on the ceiling. I was being pushed and pushed, and I could only move my hands. I was frantically trying to make sense of what was happening to me. 'Oh dear God, I've turned into an Indian mystic, and I am now levitating!' It's funny but that's really what went through my head" Mary explained. It did not take long for Mary to realize that she was not having some sort of spiritual event as she initially presumed. "I looked down to my left, and I saw three really small beings below me. One was only 2 ½ to 3 feet tall and the other ones were maybe 3 feet tall. They were in the doorway looking up at me. I remember hearing in my head, 'Oh no, oh no, not me!' I was so frightened. I began to pray, 'Hail Mary full of grace. The Lord is with me......' That's when I realized that Mother Mary isn't going to save me. Jesus isn't going to save me. I was on my own. I remember thinking that I had to get down from the ceiling. Knowing that those little beings were there, I was horrified!" Mary exclaimed. "I could hear my husband snoring loudly and wondered how he could not know this was happening. The next thing I remember was waking up the following morning and knowing that I had been on the ceiling. I have no memories of being taken by the Greys that night. It seemed that something had gone wrong during my abduction. It got botched somehow and they gave up and left me."

The Greys may have given up on taking Mary that night, or she may not remember any details if they did take her. Whatever happened that night, it did not stop them from returning. Over the course of the next three years, Mary had multiple alien abduction experiences. She and her husband began to see blue and orange colored orbs of light floating in and around their house. She would awaken and see aliens standing at the foot of her bed. She tried everything she could think of to stop the abductions, but it was to no avail. She prayed more and kept a Bible on a nightstand beside her. She even resorted to tying a silk ribbon around her big toe and the bed. When that did not work, her husband agreed to let her tie the ribbon to his foot in the hopes that he would wake up if the aliens tried to abduct her. She even convinced her husband to move their bedroom furniture to a room downstairs, since everything had happened in her upstairs bedroom. For a while, Mary thought that the move downstairs had worked. Everything was quiet. Even the large floating orbs had stopped. Mary felt a deep sense of relief, but her peace was short lived.

Mary recalled an amazing event, "It was early fall. I had fallen asleep wearing jogging shorts and a big t-shirt. I woke up, and I saw this blue misty fog come in and surround the bed. For some reason I wasn't afraid. I couldn't figure out what was happening, or why I wasn't afraid. I looked up and saw that the front door was open, and the mist was going out the front door. I got up, walked outside, and followed the mist even though I was barefoot and only wearing my gym shorts and t-shirt. I looked to my right, and I saw this perfectly round light floating over the garden. It looked like a stationary flat light, almost like a pancake. Then I looked straight ahead at my water well, and I saw this very large, muscular creature standing there in the mist. It looked like it had no neck. I still felt no fear. I called out to it, 'who are you and what are you doing here?' I asked. He wouldn't completely show himself to me. All I could see was the outline of his body. Then I saw him use what looked like a modern day tablet device. I could see from the light emitting that he was pressing it and moving images around just like we do on our tablets. Keep in mind that this happened back in the early 90's, long before we had anything like this. He had human like hands with these long, sharp fingernails that looked like talons."

Did the unusual looking figure sense that Mary was not afraid of him? Maybe, he had used mind control to ease her fear. Whatever the case, it replied to her question. Mary spoke out loud, but the creature replied telepathically. He said that he was a scientist and was collecting data. He began walking away, and Mary followed him still asking questions. He continued to walk around the property and seemed to be using the tablet device to gather data. She was shown a symbol that looked like a triangle with a little snake in it and was told to remember it. When the creature announced that it was time for him to go, Mary asked him not to leave. She had felt no fear during this encounter and actually felt that this being had been nice to her. Up until this point in her life, Mary's alien encounters had been with the Greys. This night marked the beginning of her experiences with the Reptilians.

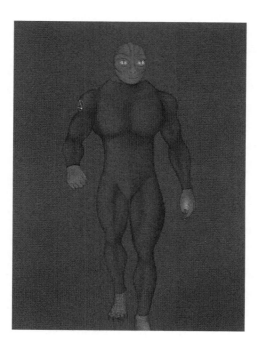

Reptilian at Mary's house
Artist – David Chace

Mary told her husband about the encounter and described the tablet device to him that the Reptilian was holding. That marriage ended, but she remarried and also told her new husband what she had witnessed that night. Years later when the first tablets came out, her husband called her at work to tell her about them. After his call she went online and did a search for them. She was shocked to see that we had developed a similar device as the Reptilian was using. As our own technology advanced, Mary observed it getting to the point where we used our fingers to manipulate the images on the screen just as the large alien had done.

One of the things that caught my attention about Mary's story was a particular event that she related which was eerily similar to something that had happened to me. This was not something commonly described by other abductees. I wrote about it in my first book in the chapter titled, "We Want Your Sex." To my knowledge, I was the first abductee to ever publicly relate such an account. It took place in an unusual looking room on their craft and involved other humans in a large scale mind controlled sex experiment. Male and female humans were being directed to have intercourse with each other, while the Greys observed. At times, a person would be moved and matched up with someone else. Most of the unwilling captives appeared to be in a zombie-like state, conscious but, at the same time, not fully aware. When Mary first contacted me, she included a rudimentary drawing of the room where she had experienced something very similar to what I had experienced. In the drawing, I could see cot like structures on which people were lying. Thankfully, she had given a copy of this drawing to her therapist before my book was published. As a result, this therapist knew that Mary had not, simply, taken my recollection of the incident and copied it. We had never met or corresponded prior to her email after my book was published. We had no way of knowing about the other's experience with the blue mats or cots.

Mary recalled the night that she was taken to the room with the cots, "I saw one man who was on one of the cots, and he was completely nude. I, somehow, ended up on the floor and was trying to get up. When he turned to his side, I saw he was naked and had some tubes attached, but I don't remember where. He attempted to reach for me, but he appeared drugged and not "Zombie like." I remember he was around 30ish with dark brown, wavy hair. He looked Latin American. He was so drugged; he finally turned over and gave up. He seemed more disoriented then me, and that frightened me! I felt someone was watching me, but I had no idea who or what. It was just an odd knowing. I then realized I was completely naked on the floor. I felt exposed, vulnerable, scared, confused and in shock, all at the same time. I didn't, however, see anyone engaged in sexual activity at all. I had absolutely no idea why I was without my clothes."

Mary continued, "Then, I tried to move and could not. I was aware because I remember wondering why all these cots were coming out of the wall. I could see a large tank with bubbles behind the cots. While I was viewing this, a man approached me. I knew this man. I leaned up and started snapping my fingers in front of my body like a crazy person and yelling, 'Hey! It's me!' He was naked and was staring straight ahead as if he didn't see me. He was like a robot, controlled, emotionless, and uncaring. In this "Zombie-like" state, he kept looking in front of him. He, then, got on his knees, grabbed my kneecaps, and began pulling them apart. That's when I remember thinking 'Oh My God, he's going to try to have sexual intercourse with me!' I panicked. He kept pulling at my knees, and, of course, I fought back. He just continued staring forward, as if he didn't even see me. I began saying his name over and over very quickly because I thought he would just snap out of this. I was trying to scream, but I could not."

"No matter what I did, he continued. This is the first time I'm sharing these details with someone other than my therapist. I guess I had to get it out. It still bothers me on many levels. I still feel betrayed; although, I know he would never do that to me in a waking state. When it was over, I just hugged him. There we were naked on the floor. He'd done this to me, and I was horrified. What's even stranger was that I was crying and hugging him when it was over. I knew this was not something he would do. He said to me plainly and without emotion, 'They need more hybrids.' That's when I freaked out and began sobbing. I don't know if the man on the other cot saw this, but I do know he reached out to attempt to help me before it occurred. I do, to some extent, feel embarrassed and ashamed. In time, I'm hoping that emotion will go."

It is rare that two individuals remember such unusual circumstances of a controlled sexual procedure like Mary and I did. Although very similar, these events happened at different times and with others. Mary also told me of a reoccurring dream of being in a room with other humans. The male humans appeared to be in some sort of trance like state similar to what we both have witnessed during the forced sexual experiment. She recalled that she was unable to move but could see with her peripheral vision other activity taking place in the room. Different human male partners were having sex with her one after the other. She said they all were devoid of emotion and all looked above her head and never directly at her when they were on top of her. To her, it seemed as if they were not fully aware of what they were doing. The men were average size and weight with short dark hair. They looked so much alike they could have been brothers. Mary's description of these men sounded very much like the men I had seen during the sexual experiments in which I was subjected. Interestingly enough, they also closely resembled the human men I have seen working for the Greys. I perceived them to be clones, perhaps, created by the Greys or some other alien species. Nevertheless, I found uncanny similarities between Mary's account of these sexual experiments and my account. This seemed to go beyond mere coincidence.

Many of us, who have had multiple encounters with an alien species, have been subjected to various kinds of sexual experimentation and procedures. When these memories surfaced, it was humiliating, embarrassing, and self-defeating. These sexual incidents were forced. Most of the procedures were related to our human reproductive system, but some dealt with the psychological and emotional aspects of sexual intercourse. These events included alien rape, sex with hybrids, semen and egg extractions, and sex with other humans as described in Mary's account. These events were not a one-time event, and the victims knew that it would happen again in some form.

Another common denominator, prevalent among abductees, is encountering the resulting consequences of these sexual experiments – alien hybrids. The human attributes of the alien hybrids vary, but they almost always appear human like. Meetings between the human abductee and the alien hybrid are invariably arranged. The human subject is told that the hybrid child is his. In most cases, I believe this is true. Sometimes an adult hybrid will present the young hybrid offspring to the human mother or father and encourage the human parent to interact with the hybrid child. This interaction is an important step for the aliens to learn how to raise this hybrid child who differs both physically and psychologically from them. As such, they closely monitor both the emotional and physical interactions between the hybrid child and the human parent.

Often, the human rejects the notion that this being is their offspring. This was the case with me when presented with the small female hybrid child whose image graces the cover of my first book. The emotional impact of these meetings is profound. It does not seem natural to accept the strange looking person as your own. Eventually, I bonded with the child, and I have longed to see her again. I have wondered what happened to her. Have I seen her again? Is she living among us? She did not look that much different than a human child. I wonder if she remembers me. Sometimes I see someone who reminds me of her, and I smile. Perhaps, she is aware of me. I do know that I am not the only Experiencer who has had to deal with the odd sense of loss as a result of meeting one of these alien/human hybrid children. Many, who have shared this experience, report feeling a strong maternal bond even though the species is not entirely human. Others are so repulsed by the alien/hybrid child that they become frightened by it. This was Mary's experience.

She recalled that horrifying night, "My husband and I were driving home from Thanksgiving dinner. It was raining and there was lots of traffic. We were both really tired. My husband looked at me and said, 'you know, I would just really like to turn off.' I said, 'me too'. He asked me to find Highway 1. I did, and we turned off on Highway 1. The last thing I remember was a wobbly type sensation, and the next thing I remember was being alone on some kind of craft. I didn't know what the hell was going on. I couldn't find my husband. I was still in my dress. I began walking down this hallway, and everything was round. I saw lots of pink colors everywhere. Then I began to wonder why I was getting so much freedom. I had never had that much freedom before. I turned to my left, and I saw two other humans sitting there with no expression on their faces. They were sitting on what looked like plastic benches. Then I saw five men there, but all seemed to be out of it. They were all about the age of 30. They were all wearing jeans except one guy who was in a suit. They looked at me but said nothing. So I asked them, 'who are you?' They wouldn't answer me, so I just kept walking. I kept thinking to myself how weird it was that I had so much freedom. Then I saw this little hole in the side of the wall. It was some kind of a pipe. I got into the hole and slid down it. When I came out of the hole, I saw windows and three tiny chairs. Sitting in one of those chairs was a type of Grey. I got extremely angry and said, 'Oh it's you, I'm going to kill you!' I lunged for him, but I didn't make it. I found myself moving very slowly like I didn't have gravity. I heard him, in my head, telling me that I wasn't special in any way, and he could squash me like an ant. I was horrified. At that point, I thought I was going to die. He let me know that he could kill me with a thought. I don't know why I felt so much rage for the creature, but I knew there was nothing that I could do about it. I just wanted to get away from it, so I turned and tried to leave the room. He did nothing to stop me from leaving. I made it into another room, and I fell on the floor. As I started to stand, I saw a Reptilian, a couple of Greys, and three hybrid looking infants. The Reptilian looked at me, and I started crying and begging God to help me. I was hysterical and he asked me to calm down."

"The aliens were standing by this black instrumental panel," Mary recalled. "The Reptilian looked at me and said, 'you have a choice.' 'You can have your life and all that's happening in it now, or you can have all the riches you want.' I told him that I didn't want riches. I only wanted to know what was happening to me and why. He then asked me what I wanted right then. I told him that I wanted the little ones to go away. He told me that they wouldn't hurt me but agreed to make them leave. Then he pushed one of the hybrid infants and said, 'it is a success.' Two of them were walking, and one looked like he was crawling. They were yellowish brown in color. They had almost human looking eyes. They had frog like skin, and their bellies were a lighter color. They had fingers with small suction cups on the tips. They were less than two feet tall and had no hair. They looked part Reptilian, part human, and part frog. One came up to me and said, 'she's here; she's here.' It sounded like a little kid. One of the other ones was crawling on me, but I told him to get off of me. They were so excited and happy that I was there with them. They all kept laughing and making giggling sounds. One of them was touching my knee with its fingers, and I could feel the suction cup attaching to me knee. I reached down and pulled it off of me. I didn't like it, and I kept telling them to stop and get away." That's when the smallest said, 'She doesn't want us. She doesn't like us.' I felt like it was hurt by my response to them."

"The next thing I remember was standing next to my husband. We were standing by a creature I had never seen before. I begged him to not take my memories this time. He replied, 'as you wish.' He then took out a long needle type instrument and tapped my husband on the side of his neck with it. I saw his head go over. Then we woke up in our car in front of our house. My husband got out of the car, and he looked up and said, 'hey look at the tree owls.' I started to hyper-ventilate because I didn't see any owls. I saw three Greys. I rushed in the house and screamed at him to follow me. A bit later, he asked me if I remembered what happened. He said that he remembered me asking the creature to let us remember. We were so upset by what had happened to us that night. We couldn't sleep and stayed up the rest of the night."

Mary's sketch of the laughing hybrid children

Mary's encounter with the odd looking alien hybrids was not a pleasant one. Even though the hybrid children were nice to her, she could not bring herself to accept them. This was not the only time in Mary's life that she was shown alien hybrid children. She was also shown more human looking hybrid babies that exhibited signs of high intelligence for their age. She felt more of a maternal bond with those hybrids. Like many other abductees, Mary wondered if they were hers, and she came to terms with the idea that she would probably never know the answer.

Chapter 6

Unfriendly Skies

I was born and raised in a small village in Pennsylvania, approximately 100 miles northeast of Cleveland, Ohio. My family and I lived on forty acres of land which was predominately woods. The area was strictly farmland, and our house was located on a dirt road off of a state route. My first memory of an alien encounter was when I was 7 years old. My younger brother and I were playing in the woods behind our house one evening. It was close to dusk. We heard a strange noise beside us and looked up to see a grey bald man with big eyes. He stared at us for a moment, and then he turned and went into the woods. We both felt that we were being pulled to follow him. My brother, who was 5, wanted to follow him, but my mother was calling us to come in for dinner. We told her what we saw, and she said to stop making up stories. To this day, my brother has refused to talk about it.

My next memory happened when I was 12. I was in my room which was on the second floor. We had a sloping roof adjacent to my bedroom window. I was sitting at my desk studying when I heard a tapping at my window. I turned to look and, just as I did, a blinding light shone into my room. I couldn't see anything. The next thing I remembered was my dad knocking on my door telling me to get up for school. I didn't mention it to my parents at that time, but I knew something had happened. A few nights later I was again in my room; it was about 10 pm. I glanced out the window. I noticed a strange glow about three or four stories above the roof of our house. I watched it hover for a minute or so and then slowly lower to near roof level. I couldn't move. I was literally frozen to the spot. The glow got stronger and stronger until I couldn't bear to keep my eyes open. After I closed my eyes, I could feel a warmness surrounding me. I felt lifted up, and I couldn't feel the floor. The next thing I knew, I was lying on my bed. I looked at the clock on my nightstand. It said 3:42 am. I didn't remember nearly 6 hours.

These encounters occurred off and on for the next few years. I never told anyone about them. I knew no one would believe me. I had gotten flashes of images since my first encounter. Some were images of me in a room with a lot of strange machines, and I was hooked up to them. Some were in a clear pod like device with lights flashing in it. I saw images of the Grey beings moving around me and examining me. Some were different looking. They had some human traits like smaller eyes, and a few had blue or green eyes. A few were taller than the Greys around them. I also have had flashes of being walked through hallways that had no doors or windows. I could hear the humming that I have heard on other occasions. These memory flashes often come when I least expect it. They have come when I was reminded of something or when I felt stressed.

I married in 1982 and had a child in 1983. After I had my son, the encounters started up again. At that time, I was living in the same area where I grew up. My husband was a paramedic and worked 24 hour shifts. One night my son was staying at his grandmothers, and I was alone in the house. I was in bed reading and heard a strange noise outside. It sounded like a low frequency hum. It gradually got louder and louder. I got out of bed to investigate, and I felt warmness and, what I can only describe as, a heartbeat in my ears. The air felt like a warm blanket had been wrapped around me. As I felt that warmness, I realized that I couldn't move. My eyes involuntarily shut, and I heard a voice in my head say, "Do not open your eyes." I felt weightless. I'm not sure how long this lasted, but I knew I wasn't alone. I woke up the next morning very ill. I was shaky, weak, and vomiting profusely. I remained this way for the next few days.

These encounters continued for the next couple of years. I always felt like I was being followed. In 1988 I discovered I was pregnant. I was extremely ill during the first 5 months. I was about 6 months along when they came again, and this time they took me with them. I awoke strapped to a table with my legs up and spread. I was naked. I could see around me. There were devices I didn't recognize and five aliens in the room. One appeared to be giving commands. I could see his face while he looked down between my legs. I felt pain, intense pain. I didn't scream. I'm not sure why. I looked up into the eyes of the one holding one of my arms, and he spoke into my thoughts. He said, "Forget the pain" and placed his hand over my eyes. The next thing I remembered was waking up covered in what I can only describe as a foul smelling slime. I was in a huge cavernous space with notches in the walls with bodies lying in them. Like me, they were naked and looked asleep. I started to crawl down from my notch and started to slide around in the slime. At the bottom, I saw what looked like bumps in the pool of slime. When I got to the pool, I could see that they were bodies. They weren't exactly human, but looked kind of human. As I waded around them, I was grabbed from behind. The next thing I knew, I woke up in my bed, and it was morning. I went into the bathroom and realized that I didn't look 6 months pregnant anymore. I ran back into the bedroom to check the sheets. They were clean. I called my husband and told him to meet me at the hospital. After the doctor examined me, he said that I showed no signs of ever being pregnant. He was baffled because he had just done a sonogram the week before. They had taken my baby! It was very similar to your experience when "they" took the fetus from your girlfriend. My husband accused me of doing something to cause a miscarriage. I couldn't explain to him what had happened. He would have had me committed. This experience resulted in a divorce. I moved to Chicago in 1992 to work as a flight attendant and to try and put some distance between me and what had happened.

The encounters continued there for the next three years. I was on an overnight in Milwaukee, WI one night. I was in a hotel room when I was visited. I awoke to find one of them sexually assaulting me. I couldn't move at all. I could feel him and see his torso, but that was all. I didn't know how long it lasted. I woke up when the alarm went off. I looked at the sheet and saw a weird substance on it. What I found really interesting about that particular encounter was that a pilot crew from Northwest Airlines reported a UFO sighting late that night in the area. I had two similar encounters like the one in Milwaukee within the next few months. I kept showing positive pregnancy results, and then a few months later I would show that I had never been pregnant.

In 1995 I moved to the city where I currently live. Shortly after I moved here, I woke up one morning with small wires embedded in my skin – in my arms, chest, legs, torso, head and even a few in my back. I called an acquaintance of mine, who worked for a metal company, to see if he could analyze the wires and determine the kind of metal it was. I put the wires in a small glass container, and I hid it in my freezer. I went on a trip and returned three days later to discover my apartment had been broken into. After surveying the damage, I realized the only thing missing was the jar of wires from my freezer. In 2010, I had a partial thyroidectomy due to tumors. During the surgery my doctor discovered I had two thyroid glands and had evidence of a previous surgery there. I have never had any surgery in that area prior to 2010. I never did find out who took the wires and my acquaintance has disappeared. My last encounter was 6 months ago. I lost almost 9 hours one evening. I keep getting flashes of memories. This area has had a lot of recent UFO sighting reports. I know this was lengthy, but after seeing you share your story, I felt compelled to contact you. It is such a relief to know that there are others who understand what I have been through. I thank you for your time and for listening.

The above copy was the content of the first email I received from a lady that I will refer to as Karen. She, too, has asked that her real identity remain hidden, as she fears her revelations would adversely affect her job as a flight attendant. I was moved by her honesty in revealing her terrifying alien abduction events to me. She had seen me on a television show. Even though my contact information was not listed, she felt compelled to find me and tell me her story. As I read through the brief account of her traumatic experiences, I could not help but notice the numerous similarities between her experiences and my own experiences with the visitors. As it turned out, there would be more to come.

Karen's first encounter with a Grey happened when she was only 7. I was just 5 years old when I was first taken, the same age as

Karen's brother at the time of their incident. It is not uncommon for children of this age to have their first experience. Ages 3 to 7 are the most prevalent ages for alien abductions to begin, especially for the "lifers." Karen's mother reacted in much the same way as mine did when she was told about the "grey, bald guy with big eyes." It is unfortunate that many parents, of children who are being taken, dismiss it as "imaginary friends" or think that their children are "making up stories." Of course, that does happen, but there are times when that is not the case. I cannot emphasize this enough. I always advise parents, whose children talk of strange experiences or visitors, to hear them out and listen intently to their stories. Parents also need to keep a close eye on them for any unusual marks or behavior changes associated with their stories. Many times, children will simply give up; they think no one will ever believe them. Then, they are left to deal with these terrifying experiences on their own.

I wanted to learn more about Karen's encounters. I emailed her and asked if I could call and talk further about her experiences. I also asked if I could interview her for this book. She graciously agreed. In a subsequent phone call to Karen, she recalled other details of her life that closely paralleled my own. She lived in a rural area when her first encounter occurred, just as I did. She said she rarely watched TV back then because there were only three television channels. Like me, she had never been exposed to any kind of visual representation of an alien or anything related to the subject. Needless to say, her first encounter left her petrified. She said that her family used to burn their trash in an old barrel in the back of their house. When she was asked to take out the trash, she would bribe her brother to do it because she was too afraid to walk out there alone, especially at dusk. She always felt like she was being watched. I was very much like that as a child. All children have some fear of the dark or of being alone. Those, who have been visited or taken, experience that fear at an entirely different level. As children, we did not know why we were so afraid. We just knew that the fear was very real.

During our phone conversation, Karen recalled another childhood memory that sounded hauntingly familiar. "I shared a bedroom on the second floor of our house with my brother and my sister. We were all within two years of age of each other. I remember my Mother having an issue with me. She couldn't figure out why I kept waking up with blood on my sheets. We couldn't figure out where it was coming from. I would go to bed, and the next morning I would wake up and find blood. It would either be on my pillow or somewhere on the bed. My Mom was getting frustrated with me. She kept asking me what I was doing. They checked my mouth, thinking that maybe I was biting my tongue but could never find any source or reason for the blood on my sheets." I went through a similar experience during my childhood. Even as an adult, I have awoken and found blood on my pillow case. Now, I have an understanding as to the cause. These are the types of physical signs of an alien abduction that are often hidden in plain sight and dismissed when an explanation cannot be found.

Karen also wrote of hearing a low frequency hum just before being taken one night. As I stated in a previous chapter, I too have heard these low frequency hums many times, and they were always a precursor to an abduction event. Sometimes I would start to hear the hum a day or two before, and sometimes, it would happen that night. I have never found out what it is or what purpose it serves. It is a low frequency hum, and it pulsates in a particular rhythm. Others around me do not hear it. It appears that only other abductees can hear it.

A couple of years ago, I heard it over the course of two days. I knew something was going to happen. A sense of dread came over me. Sure enough, I was taken. I woke up feeling very nauseated just like Karen. That day I contacted three other abductees, two in middle Tennessee and one in Kentucky. I asked them if they had heard any unusual sounds recently. All three described the same low frequency hum. Two of them believed they had been taken either the same night as me or the previous night. Both woke up feeling sick. It was possible that the third could have been taken and just did not remember it. In addition to hearing the hum before abduction, Karen also said that she has heard it on board a craft.

She further described the hum. "The hum I hear often, too often. When it is really strong I get nauseous. I have seen doctors for the nausea, and they have tested me for virtually everything that it could possibly be, and nothing helps. I also have vertigo to the point where I lose my balance. This got worse after the baby was taken." Karen went on to describe other effects of alien abduction. "I always have the feeling of being followed. I have accepted it. I actually became a licensed private investigator in my state because it made me feel better, and I felt a little bit in control. I know it's futile, but it helps me cope. I also belong to a paranormal group based in my area. That helps me cope as well."

Some would claim that Karen is simply paranoid or suffering from some sort of mental illness. That is not the case. A large number of people, who have been taken, also feel they are being followed or watched on a regular basis. Perhaps, it stems from the implants. Maybe the implants trigger something in our brains that make us feel that we are being observed and monitored. It could also be a symptom of Post Traumatic Stress Disorder. When you become aware that you have been taken against your will, a kind of paranoia does develop. No one knows what it is like to live every day of your life knowing that "they" will come again and wondering if this will be the day. Most alien abductees suffer from sleep disorders too. Abductees are afraid to go to sleep because they might get taken during sleep. I have experienced this countless times. I am also a very light sleeper which I attribute to my past encounters. Karen mentions that, although she has accepted that she is being monitored, she still has taken measures to give herself what small amount of control she can. She admits that she believes her efforts are futile. I admire that she is doing things to empower herself in our world. It is imperative for anyone who has gone through these kinds of overwhelming experiences to do whatever he or she can in order to cope. Empower yourself in whatever way you feel works. Gaining the courage to tell others is also a major step in the healing process. I know how difficult it must have been for Karen to contact me and tell me details of her abductions. It is not easy to relive these experiences. I am happy that Karen has accepted these experiences. Acceptance is one of the most difficult things to achieve on the journey to healing. You cannot succumb to being a victim.

Karen endured so many horrific sexual acts. I felt strongly that she must have been shown the end results. I asked her if she was ever shown an alien hybrid child. "I remember a time shortly after my fetus was removed that I was taken again. I remember waking up and being handed a bundle that was wrapped in strange fabric. I was told telepathically to open the bundle. I did, and it was a very strange, reptilian looking infant. It had a rigid bump along the top of its head. It had very small blue eyes with no eyelashes or eyebrows. It was greenish/dark gray in color. The fingers were very long and had what appeared to be four joints. The mouth looked somewhat like a lizard. The nose was tiny holes. I couldn't see any more of the body due to the fabric. The bundle was then taken out of my hands, and I remember starting to scream at the top of my lungs. The next thing I knew I was standing in the middle of my kitchen. Another memory happened on more than one occasion. I haven't pinpointed any time frame; although, I do feel that it was during the time of my fetus removal. I remember being submerged in a very strange liquid that resembled jelly. It was very warm. I remember feeling it ebb and flow over my body and feeling a pulsating sensation that terrified me. I was actually breathing this liquid."

I believe Karen was being used as a breeder for both the Greys and the Reptilians. I do not mean to sound harsh or disrespectful to Karen by using the word "breeder." The reality is we are their breeders. Her description of the hybrid child she saw seemed to indicate that it was a Human/Reptilian hybrid. I asked her if she could remember any more details about the being that raped her in the hotel room. A Grey would not have been able to have intercourse with a female of its own species, let alone a human female. I suspected it was either a Reptilian or a hybrid. Karen said, "The being in my hotel room was different from the Greys that I usually saw. His head was a bit smaller. He had smaller eyes, and they were bluish in color. He spoke to me through my thoughts and calmed me. I felt a euphoria wash over me, and all I could see was him. I was unable to move or resist him after that." After hearing more details about the alien assailant, it sounded like he could have been a hybrid. The description reminded me of the female Grey/human hybrid woman who was sent into a room to have sex with me. If the Greys used human males to impregnate their female hybrids, then it made sense that they would use male hybrids to impregnate human females. It also could have been a full blooded Reptilian, and

Karen's memory was, possibly, a screen memory of a less hideous creature. After hearing various accounts of sexual experiences with these beings, it was, most likely, an alien hybrid attempting to impregnate Karen to further propagate the hybrid species.

Another interesting thing that Karen revealed to me during our conversation was that her father had also been an alien abductee. "My dad passed away in December of 2013. Before he passed, I learned something that I did not know. I went home in March of that year to visit him. He had rectal cancer, and it had spread all through his body. He knew he was going to die. One day while I was talking to him, he admitted that he had had experiences. I didn't even bring it up; he brought it up. I was floored! I was sitting on the edge of his bed listening to him. No one else was around. He told me about years of alien experiences. It was almost like it was spilling out of him. He knew his time was ending, and he knew that I was a paranormal investigator. I think he knew that I would be open to hearing about it."

"He was 72, and guys like him just didn't talk about that stuff. He talked about how he had been taken up in a craft numerous times. He said he had seen them, and they had done things to him. He talked about the little guys with the big eyes. He wasn't very articulate. It was almost like it was coming out so fast that he couldn't keep up with it. He was trying to tell me everything. I felt like there was a sense of urgency within him, and he desperately wanted to get it all out. I didn't want to interrupt him because it was just pouring out of him. He used to work for the railroad. There were times when he would be taken from his car after coming home from work at night. He would be sitting in his car in front of our house. Hours would go by, and he would find himself still sitting there. He said that there were times when he saw a craft near our home. I had as well as a child. All of this came out in the open. I had gone my whole life and had no idea that my Dad was having these kinds of experiences."

I was not surprised to learn that Karen's dad had also been taken throughout his life. I have said it many times before, and I will say it again here. Once the aliens find a certain set of genetic markers that they favor within a family line, they will stay with that line for generations. I have found this to be true in many abduction cases;

especially, when the abductee has been taken numerous times over the course of his or her lifetime. Yet, the big question still remains. What parameters dictate which genetic code they like and why? Many Native American cultures have long standing beliefs that their ancestors are from the stars. Could this belief be true? If so, it could possibly explain why so many abductees have some Native American blood flowing in their veins. There are also a large number of people of Celtic decent. When you combine the two, it seems to be a highly favored DNA mix, at least for the Greys. Such is the case with me. I am a mix of Irish, English and Native American. Karen told me that she had researched her own ethic background and discovered that she is Native American and Scottish.

I could only imagine the sense of urgency Karen's father must have felt trying to recount a lifetime of alien abduction experiences in a short amount of time. It is so sad that he carried that heavy burden with him for so many years. There is no telling how many other abductees are out there carrying that same burden with them. They remain silent because they are afraid of the consequences they might face if their truth was known. The magnitude of this phenomenon cannot be measured. There are untold numbers of people who have memories of alien encounters but remain forever silent about them. At this point in time, there is no way to know how many Experiencers there are. Suffice it to say, there is a very large number of human beings, on this planet, being taken against their will by either an extraterrestrial or ultra terrestrial life form. The exact number is irrelevant. The concern should be that it is happening at all.

Even in this day and age, the sexual aspects of these alien encounters is still taboo. That fact alone is absolutely mind boggling. Why is it so often overlooked and ignored when it is one of the most important parts of the alien abduction phenomenon? Many people, who have had an abduction experience, shy away from talking about any procedures or experiments of a sexual nature. I understand that it can be humiliating and embarrassing to put oneself in a vulnerable position by talking about it. I have done it. I know what it is like. I have spoken personally and publically to others who have been forced into these sexual acts. I have encouraged them to speak about it. If this has happened to you, you had no way to stop it. You were under the control of your captors, as were other humans that may have been forced upon you. The aliens are insensitive to the psychological repercussions that stem from their procedures and experiments. It is important to share with others the sexual details of your encounters. It helps both you and them. It also helps the general public to better understand and hopefully empathize with people who have lived through this reality.

Numerous alien abductees have shared their experiences with me. I began to see a trend among those who spoke openly about the sexual aspects of their experiences. Striking similarities began to surface. Karen discussed things she remembered from her childhood that she thought related to her abduction experiences. She said that, as a child, she was painfully shy and withdrawn. So much so, that she was put on medication. Then, she felt something change within her. "It felt like it happened overnight. I became extremely sexual. I won't say promiscuous, but I became extremely curious. This was even before puberty. I felt like I knew things that I shouldn't know about sex. It was really weird because I almost felt like I was being told things. I was never exposed to anything, but I knew things that the average 10 or 11 year old should not know."

She continued, "When I hit puberty, I began to have this reoccurring dream, but it was not a dream. In it, I was lying on a table. I couldn't really feel anything but I knew that someone was having sex with me. I also knew that I was not alone there. I was having sex with one after another. I couldn't see anything else around me, but I was lying down. There was a guy on top of me, and it continued, one after another. In my thoughts I begged, 'please stop!' Then the next thing I remembered was waking up." Karen recalled more about her traumatic experience, "I could see their faces, but they were not looking at me during the sex act. They were all so stoic looking; it was almost like they were wearing a mask. I was unable to move. I felt paralyzed." I asked Karen what she remembered about her environment. "I was in a room, and, through my peripheral vision, I could tell that there was other stuff happening. I wasn't able to turn and look. I was being controlled and couldn't move. It was like some sort of sexual assembly line. All the men looked very similar to each other. They were completely devoid of emotion. They were looking above my head and not even looking directly at me."

As Karen revealed more details of her event, I noticed the shocking similarities between what happened to her and what happened to me in the room with blue cots. It also sounded very much like what Mary experienced and described in the previous chapter. I asked Karen if she remembered any more details about the men who had, for lack of a better word, raped her. "They were just your average Joe kind of guys. They had brown or dark hair. To me, they looked so much like each other. They almost looked like brothers," Karen recalled. The description of the men that Karen described closely matched the male humans that I witnessed during my encounters. I have also seen and communicated with male humans who appeared to be working with, or for, the Greys. These men also looked very much like the men Karen described. Karen noted that the men looked so much alike that they could be brothers. I felt the same way about the men I saw, especially the ones working alongside the Greys. As I have stated previously, they may have been clones. Have Alien races created human clones? Are they using them as workers and breeders? Is it possible that all the men in the group sex event had similar DNA and were chosen for that reason? During that same event, I also noticed that all of the women had dark brown or black hair as well. We may have the DNA they want and carry similar physical traits because of it. I do believe, however, they have created human clones and are using them for various purposes.

It is known and, for the most part, accepted that fetuses are being taken from female abductees. Some of these women will endure this trauma many times throughout their life. It seems that the aliens decide if a woman in their hybrid program will be allowed to carry a child to full term and deliver. For some women, this never happens. Others will eventually give birth to a child of their own. This is allowed so that a particular line of genetics can continue, thus enabling the aliens to have a continual supply of human mothers. Such was the case with Karen. She eventually gave birth to twins. But even the birth of the twins was filled with unusual circumstances and mystery. Karen explained, "When my son was delivered, he was not only perfect but scored a 10 on the Apgar Test given immediately after the baby exits the womb and again 5 minutes later. The doctor and nurse both said that a 10 upon womb exit was literally unheard of. He was pink, and babies aren't pink until they start to breathe oxygen. The doctor asked me to push again, and the other baby was delivered. It wasn't breathing, and they could not revive it. The doctor and nurse refused to let me or my husband see the baby; this was unusual especially since it was full term."

"We were living in Pennsylvania. In the state of Pennsylvania, any stillborn baby over five months is required to be named and buried or cremated," Karen explained. "The doctor told the nurse to take the baby into the other room and to let no one enter the room. I was in shock from the delivery and was so distracted with my new son that I didn't realize the strangeness at the time. I also had three placentas, which the doctor told the nurse to take into the room with my stillborn child. After I settled back into my room, my husband and I asked to see our deceased baby so we could say goodbye. We got the run around for a few hours. A hospital administrator came in and told us that there had been a mix-up, and our baby had inadvertently been sent to a funeral home. We were never able to track it down. We were both young when this happened and didn't think to pursue it any further. My son will be 30 in June. He's never broken a bone or suffered a sprain even though he was active with baseball, surfing, running and so forth. He skipped grades in school, and his IQ was tested at 204. He is currently completing his PHD at a university where he works over a staff of nine. He makes me wonder…"

Those of you who read *"Children of the Greys"* are familiar with the mysterious scars that I have on my body. I wrote in detail about finding them and presented photos of them in the book. The unexplained puncture marks, I have, are actually quite common among abductees. The scars across my spine are not. I have only come across one other case in which a male abductee mentioned finding a scar on his lower back. He, too, had no idea how it got there. As I wrote earlier, I have never received a feasible explanation as to what caused my scars even though several doctors have examined them over the years. When Karen began to talk about her unusual back scars, I was stunned.

"This was a shock to me!" Karen exclaimed. "In the summer of 2013 I went in for some injections in my lower back for pain. I was lying on the table with all the bright lights on and everything. All of a sudden the doctor says to me, 'When did you have surgery on your back?' I was very surprised to hear him ask me that. I told him that I hadn't had back surgery and asked why he had asked me that. He said, 'Well, you have a scar back here.' He put his finger on it and said, 'Right here.' I was very perplexed and replied again that I had never had surgery on my back. I really didn't give it much thought after that. Then the following January, I went to a chiropractor. I was having a problem with my lower L5 S1 disc. He did adjustments and decided that I should get an MRI. When the MRI came back, it was discovered that I had a spot on my lower spine. It was round, black and about the size of a pencil eraser. The doctor did not have a clue as to what it was. It was not fatty tissue or bone. His friend, a surgeon, looked at it, and he also had no clue as to what it was." Karen's account of her scar and subsequent MRI results left me speechless. Karen and I have never met each other, and we both have unexplained scars on our back. Also, neither one of us has ever had back surgery. What were the chances of this? If one took into account our long history of alien abductions, then the odds were staggering. It appeared that our back scars, as well as other scoop and puncture marks, were a direct result of medical procedures performed on us by our alien captors. This kind of physical evidence has, all too often, been ignored by the mainstream science community.

The commonalities between Karen's case and mine did not stop there. In the summer of 2013, Karen found scoop marks and, what she described as, injection marks on her body. The marks had not been present the previous night. She noticed them while showering the next morning. The injection marks left a blood bruise under her skin, much like when having blood drawn. Karen noted that the injection marks healed. Two weeks later, she woke up, and the injection marks had returned in the same spot. The process repeated once more, but this time it happened after a period of three weeks. The marks were again in the same spot. I experienced similar marks in 2014, but my incident happened while I was awake as I described previously in this book. From her description, our marks sounded identical. The main difference was the location of the injection mark sites. Mine were on the top of my right hand while Karen's were on the inner part of her right arm.

Karen's scar on lower back

Close up of scar on my lower back

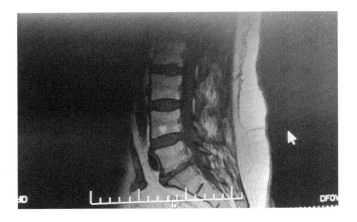

Karen's MRI Image

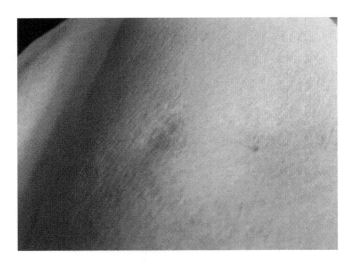

Karen's scoop marks

There is no telling how many times Karen has been impregnated and used to gestate a fetus. During her recollections, she recalled numerous times that she exhibited signs of pregnancy only to have them suddenly cease. Karen would often go to her doctor in hopes of finding out what was causing her pregnancy symptoms but to no avail. She remembered one visit specifically, "I was getting examined, and the doctor said that it looked like I had just been pregnant. I told him that I didn't think I had been pregnant, and he said, 'It looks like you were.' Then there were times that I did think I was pregnant, and I know it was taken. There were several times I woke up from an awful nightmare about it, and I was bleeding from my vagina so bad that I thought I was going to have to go to the emergency room. That was not normal for me at all. It was painful; it felt like I had been scraped and poked in my uterus. I underwent a D&C once, and I knew what that felt like. It was the same kind of feeling; it felt just like I had had a D&C. It wasn't like a cyst. It felt like I had had surgery. It wasn't cramps or anything like that. I never got cramps. It was different. I knew it wasn't that. There were so many times that something unusual was going on down there."

Karen did have one very vivid memory of a traumatic encounter that involved a hybrid and was definitely related to her missing fetuses and pregnancy issues. "I was taken. When I came to, I found myself lying there with my legs spread. I knew that something was going on, but I couldn't feel anything from my waist down. This happened in 1993. I'll never forget it!" She exclaimed. "I was in a dark room and I had this dark fabric across my knees. I remembered looking around the room, and there was nothing else there. I saw a dull light in front of me. All of a sudden I saw a head. It reminded me of a gynecologist because I had my legs up in stirrup type things, in that position. I looked up and saw the head. It was not an actual Grey. It looked like a hybrid. He was taller and very thin. His eyes were really dark. He did not have much of a nose and mouth. He was wearing a dark colored shirt. He looked at me, but I couldn't feel anything that he was doing. I couldn't feel anything below my waist. It didn't seem like he was having sex with me. It was more like he was implanting something or taking something out. It was more clinical than something sexual. He was moving around and would turn to the side a little bit. He, occasionally, looked up at me and then looked back down. I didn't know if he wanted some kind of reaction or what," Karen recalled. She continued, "I just kept looking at him. In my head I'm thinking, 'what are you doing, what are you doing?' I wanted to scream! I was just about to let out a scream when I felt this hand right on top of my forehead, and I blacked out. I didn't see who it was."

It was difficult listening to Karen as she described this terrifying experience. It must be hard to imagine the myriad of emotions that races through one's mind during such an event, unless you have experienced it yourself. All of Karen's many experiences with the visitors add a new burden for her. All experiences, that an abductee goes through, affect him or her psychologically, physically, or both psychologically and physically. Karen's remarkable story continues. Like me, she is a lifer. There will be no reprieve or escape. The high strangeness continues. Not long after my phone interview with her for this book, I received an email from Karen. Here is the brief but incredible email. "I just wanted to send you a quick email to let you know something that just happened a few minutes ago. I have my television on, and I'm watching a movie. My remote control is about 10 feet away from me. All of a sudden my TV changes the channel, on its own, to the History Channel. It is an episode of Ancient Aliens, the Alien Breeders episode, and there you are telling your story! Crazy, huh?" Maybe not, Karen, maybe not......

Chapter 7

ALIEN SEXPLOITS

I have known Sandy Nichols for almost seven years. We met, by chance, at a small UFO conference that was held in the middle Tennessee area. Soon after the conference, Sandy invited Rena and me to his house for dinner. Sandy was cordial and accommodating, as was his wonderful wife Sherrie. As the evening progressed, the conversation quickly shifted to UFOs. It was then I learned that Sandy was also an alien abductee. That night Sandy told us about some of his experiences. Tears rolled down this man's face as he recalled some of his traumatic encounters. I was touched by his openness and willingness to share these harrowing events with us. As we left that night, I felt a sense of camaraderie with Sandy. He did not know it then, but I could relate to the experiences and emotions created by these other worldly encounters.

At that time, few people knew about my own lifetime of alien abductions. I was still "in the closet," so to speak. Sandy, on the other hand, had gone public in the late 1990s. I was impressed by his courage, especially after learning about the consequences he had endured for choosing to speak publically. Eventually, I began to open up to Sandy about my own abductions. We talked about our similar experiences. We also talked about the psychological effects of alien abduction. Sandy put a large punching bag in his basement, and that was where he would go and release his pent up anger. He stated that there were many times that he simply broke down, rested his head in his wife's lap, and wept. Abductees have to deal with intense emotions throughout their life. Sadly, not many consider the after effects of an alien abduction.

When you have been repeatedly taken for years, you learn mental survival skills. You use this skill set both in your regular life and during abduction events. You also accept the fact that there is a good chance that the aliens will never stop taking you. Both Sandy and I help others who are affected by these obtrusive supernatural events. Sandy set up a website to help other abductees and Experiencers. It can be found at www.alienresearchgroup.com. Sandy has no qualms talking publicly about his personal and intimate encounters. His experiences parallel my own abduction experiences. When I asked to interview him, he agreed without hesitation.

Sandy's first abduction happened when he was around the age of five. Sandy vividly remembered the event as an actual memory and not something that was recalled under hypnotic regression. I have found this to be very common, especially with the Greys. They seem to make no effort to erase or suppress the memories of children. Maybe, they know no one will believe a young child telling such a story to his or her parents. "My mother remembered me telling her about the little men who took me away in the middle of the night. She said she didn't think anything of it at the time and passed it off as my imaginary friends." This seems to be the case with many adults when their child tells them something similar. Sandy elaborated on his first incident with the visitors. "I was spending the weekend at my Grandmother's home in east Nashville with my two oldest brothers which was a rare treat. It was early morning, and I was playing war. I was commanding my troops from the raised back porch of my Grandmother's home that overlooked her small back yard. A short time into commanding, I noticed what looked like a 'round airplane' descending into the partially vacant neighborhood behind her house. When the 'round airplane' landed, I could barely see the top of it because of tall, overgrown grass in the field.

A few minutes later, two small, strange looking kids emerged from that area into my Grandmother's back yard. Instead of running into the house and telling my Grandmother, I left my lofty perch and walked into the back yard. The two kids wanted me to go with them into the field. At first, I refused but then consented to go with them. We then began to float. We floated into the field to the round airplane. The next thing I knew, I was inside the craft. I was escorted down this circular hallway into a dimly lit room where other children my age were playing with toys. I walked over to a table and picked up one of three toys. Even though I had never seen these toys before, I knew how to play with them. Two of the toys could be flown by, basically, willing them to fly. The other toy was a wand with fiber optic tubes attached to it. I could swish this toy in the air and draw multi-colored images in the air with it. The images would remain in the air for several seconds and then disappear. After this first experience, these two kids would periodically return for me, mainly at night after I had gone to bed. I enjoyed playing with them and with the toys. As I grew older, the experiences began to change. They became physically and emotionally invasive and were performed by new 'kids,' who were just as strange looking and tall."

"I remember the 'tall kids' touching my genitals while I was lying on a metal like table," Sandy recalled. "I have no idea what kind of test or medical procedure that they were doing. I do remember several times when my mother would have my father check my genital area because of blood found on my underwear. As far as I can remember, my Dad never found anything that would account for the blood. It would be years later, after two particular experiences, that I finally admitted they were messing with my genitals." He continued, "One morning I woke up at 8 a.m. after going to bed at 3 a.m. I felt an overwhelming urge to urinate. I looked down as I urinated, and I saw a scoop mark on the head of my penis. It was on the side, near the end. It was a hole about a quarter inch deep and a little smaller than a dime. The inside of the hole was black and crusty looking. I called my internal medicine doctor and went to see him. He had no idea what had transpired; he sent me to see a urologist. The urologist came in and was dumbfounded when he looked at the area." "He left and came back with another doctor," Sandy continued. "That doctor was just as perplexed. They excused themselves and came back with a third doctor and an armful of medical books. For the next hour, they examined the area thoroughly while sifting through the medical books.

They had no idea what had caused the injury, but the black, crusty lining inside the hole was the result of a cauterization procedure. They sent me home with a plastic bag of Q-tips and a tube of cream that I never used. By the next morning, the hole was completely healed. A few weeks later, I noticed a faint brown, narrow ring around the head of my penis. I wondered if this ring was some sort of an alien marking tattoo. In 2015, after 20 years, the ring began to disappear over a period of six months."

When I heard Sandy's second story, I felt hope rush from my body like a dam that had been breached. Both Sandy and I have had sperm extractions numerous times during abductions. When he mentioned what had happened after his vasectomy, I felt depressed. I too had a vasectomy several years ago. At the time, I foolishly believed that it would stop the Greys from taking me and subjecting me to these sperm extraction procedures. I was wrong. It did not stop them. Sandy recounted, "I awakened on a Saturday morning with a terrible pain in my groin area. It felt as if I had been hit with a baseball bat. Upon checking the area, I noticed a spot of blood and, what appeared to be, a puncture mark on my right testicle. There was no doubt that the pain I was experiencing was emanating from this spot, and I found out very quickly that it was sensitive to touch and cold. I showed the spot to my wife Sherrie. Sherrie, a former Captain and Flight Nurse in The United States Air Force, said the mark was similar in appearance to something akin to a hypodermic needle puncture mark. By Sunday afternoon, the pain began to subside, but the puncture mark remained. Three to four months later, I awakened to the same excruciating pain, a spot of blood, and another puncture mark. This time it was on my left testicle. For the next year, this same process occurred every three to four months and alternated between testicles. During that entire time, I tried in vain to understand what was happening to me. Then one afternoon I had a flashback."

"In my early forties I had a vasectomy," Sandy explained. "Before I had the vasectomy, I had endured many abduction experiences where the beings had taken sperm from me. This procedure would begin with the aliens causing me to have an erection. Then, a tube was placed over my penis, and sperm was literally sucked out of me. The orgasmic feeling induced by this process was second to none. Once it was over, however, I felt like I had been raped. The puncture marks were beginning to make sense. The beings could no longer use this sperm extraction process on me anymore because of the vasectomy. Now, they were resorting to removing sperm directly from my testicle using a hypodermic needle."

The sexual nature of the experiments and procedures has been a prominent factor during many abduction events. I wrote extensively about mine, and I have included other's alien sexual revelations in this book. These sexual encounters have been other worldly, but they have also involved other humans. I asked Sandy if he had ever been forced by the Greys to have sex with other humans. He replied, "Yes, but the word force is a double edge sword during these types of experiences. By double edge, I mean that the aliens would implant a strong, emotional feeling of sexual attraction in my thoughts toward human females which I then would act upon," he explained. "Under normal circumstances during non-abduction experiences, I would not have had a sexual attraction to some of these females."

Sandy recalled a particular experience with a woman he called "Julie." He chose not to reveal her real name. He has met her and does not believe that she remembers their shared sexual experience. If she has retained any memories, she has not shared them with Sandy. This is understandable considering the possible embarrassment that could occur, if the other party did not remember the event or was repulsed by the event. When listening to stories about alien experiments, it is important to take into account the emotional aftermath of these experiences on abductees. Was a bond formed by one person or the other? Was this bond real, or was it implanted by the aliens? What other emotions can be identified? If anger is present, where is it directed? It may be directed at both aliens and other humans involved in the experiment. When dealing with human emotions, especially when sex is involved, there is a myriad of possible outcomes as to how someone will accept, understand, and cope with such an event. This process is even more complicated when it is alien induced.

"Julie was sweet as she could be. She was soft spoken and a comfort to be around in troubled times," Sandy said as he described her.

"Julie and I were brought together by the Greys for the first time when we were young. This continued off and on into our early adult years. I had shared abductions with other humans before, but Julie was the only human that I was brought together with in a sexual manner. The sexual attraction induced in us by the aliens happened more than once with Julie. It began in our early adult years, but, to be honest, I had already developed a strong emotional feeling for Julie. I have since wondered if the feelings I felt for Julie were real or induced by the aliens. Since I was not married at the time, there was no guilt associated with my feelings for Julie or the enjoyment I felt being with her."

The Greys have an affinity for observing the act of sexual intercourse between the humans they bring together. I do not believe that they garner any pleasure from watching it, but, rather, they learn from monitoring it. I am sure they yearn to tap into the emotional triggers behind it. It is all a part of the process for them. I do not believe that the Greys are able to reproduce in a natural biological way like humans do. However, the alien hybrids have some human physical attributes. They are able to reproduce. This creates a problem for the Greys. They do not understand the emotional bonds created by the sex act. What creates this bond between some humans during sex? Why do some humans not feel that emotional connection? What creates the physical attraction that produces sexual arousal? Why does it not work the same between all humans? What neurons fire in the human brain during intercourse and why? What array of emotions is produced during the human sex act and what causes them? We do not think about these questions much. We just feel it. If you are an extra-terrestrial race creating a hybrid race, the answers to these questions are of the utmost importance. Even with their superior intellect, the Greys have yet to fully understand the human psyche. They control humans through implants or telepathic mind control. They place most abductees into a zombie like state and then force them to have intercourse with barely coherent strangers. How could they possibly learn about normal human sexuality and its subsequent emotions from this disastrous experiment? Have they not yet realized they are blocking the very thing they seek?

Sandy was placed with Julie numerous times over a period of

several years. Their sexual interludes were always done in front of an audience of Greys. This was the normal procedure in my case as well. Sandy and Julie never engaged in any small talk during their shared abduction experiences. They never exchanged any personal information. He knew nothing about her. He did not know where she lived, if she was married, or if she had children. Many abductees have witnessed other humans during an event. Often, there is forced sexual interaction between an abductee and other humans. This can mess with your mind. I have often wondered who these other people are. Would we recognize each other if our paths crossed here? How much do they remember? Would they say something, if they did remember? There have been times that I have met someone in person or have been contacted by someone who claims to remember seeing me during an abduction event. None, however, have ever mentioned anything sexual. The memories described have been mostly foggy. I do not discount their recollections; even though, some are not accurate. There is the possibility that some are real memories. I, too, have met people that I am sure I have seen on a craft. I know it happens.

Sandy's years of continuous shared abductions with Julie left him with an emotional attachment to her. Sandy recalled his feelings after they were separated. "Julie was a gift in my life, and the gift had been taken away. Over time, the sadness and loneliness I felt began to dissipate. He explained, "From the time I was 9 or 10 years of age, I had heard so many times that my experiences were just my imagination, I began to believe it. For years, I lived in a state of denial writing off my experiences to one thing or another, despite the fact that my abductions continued. When Julie and I were separated, I placed her into this same category. I eventually fought my way out of denial with professional counseling and regressive hypnosis to help uncover buried memories. Several years after I began this process, I received an unexpected email. I was contacted by someone named Julie. I had no idea that this person was the same Julie I had the shared abduction experiences with until several months later when we met face to face." Sandy continued, "As soon as I saw her face, I knew, and a flood of hidden memories rushed into my conscious thoughts. The revelation that descended upon me did not descend upon Julie. We still chat and see each other from time to time. To this day, I have never shared my memories with her. Until her memories are revealed to her, I will keep my secret."

Many abductees, including me, have also been placed in sexual situations with alien hybrids. This serves two purposes for the aliens. One is a possible direct impregnation from a human male to a female hybrid. The other provides an opportunity to monitor the feelings, if any, of the female hybrid towards her human sex partner. As you might expect, most of the human males do not find the female hybrids attractive and thus have no interest in having sex with them. I do not find the hybrid women repulsive. Actually, they have a pleasant demeanor. They seem serene and calm and, most likely, are being forced into this sexual situation too. The shocking part comes when you realize that you are being intimate with a creature from another world.

I asked Sandy if he had ever experienced a sexual encounter with a female alien hybrid. His answer was immediate and emphatic, "Oh yes! It involved a nefarious form of thought and visual manipulation." He related the incident. "It was a Saturday afternoon, and I had been working around the house. I finished by mid-afternoon and had time to take a quick shower and a nap before dinner. Being hot natured, I retired to an upstairs bedroom which tended to be cooler than the master bedroom downstairs. To stay cool after my shower, I did not get dressed and was nude as I quickly nodded off. The next thing I remember I was being taken by the Greys to a room. I was still nude. When I entered the room, I immediately noticed a woman standing in the room. She was also naked. The woman was so beautiful! She was every man's fantasy of the perfect woman. My desire for her was instant and overwhelming. For some reason, I felt that she desired me as much as I did her." "Without hesitation," Sandy said, "We wrapped our arms around each other in a deep embrace and kissed. Seconds later, we climbed upon this metal looking table that was in the middle of the room. I lay on my back, and the woman straddled me. The eerie silence of the room heightened the sounds of our lovemaking. What should have been a perfect moment began to feel very strange to me. The unbridled passion I felt at first began to fade. I felt uneasiness about what was transpiring. My head began to hurt, and my vision blurred."

"When my vision had cleared, my perfect woman was no more. Instead, I saw a tall female Grey!" Sandy exclaimed. "Maybe she was a hybrid, but she was definitely not the beautiful vision of human female perfection I thought she was. I immediately reached out and pushed her off of me. Half way to the floor, she stopped in mid air and righted herself. I jumped off the table and was confronted by a tall male Grey. He demanded that I get back on the table. I refused. He did not seem pleased by my defiance, and he demanded again. Once again, I refused. The next thing I knew, I was on my knees in the middle of the bedroom floor with dry heaves. The thought of having intergalactic sex with some alien creature had made me physically sick."

The Greys did not suppress Sandy's memories of the event. He was greatly bothered and confused by what had happened to him. He could not understand why they would subject him to that kind of sexual encounter. Because of his vasectomy, he could not impregnate the hybrid. Finally, the inevitable conclusion revealed itself to Sandy just as it had to me. It was a demonstration of the lovemaking process. The Greys were interested in the emotions created by the sexual act. He figured out that these clever intruders had gone inside his subconscious mind and pulled out what he perceived as his "dream woman." They then used that against him as a screen memory to achieve their prime directive. It appeared that both the Greys and Sandy learned from the incident. The next time it would not be so easy for the Greys.

Being an alien abductee can scar you for life. Those, that remember, will be psychologically affected in some way. Some experiences, not only, leave a lasting impact on your psyche but your heart as well. One such experience was when I was shown a hybrid child and told that it was mine. I was so affected by this experience that I put the image of the little hybrid girl on the cover of my first book. I do not know if more women have this experience than men or if they simply report it more. Sandy is one of the few male experiencers that have met a hybrid child. The scenario was typical in that he was told the child was his and asked to interact with the child. In fact, he was presented with two hybrid children during the same abduction experience.

Sandy recounted the event, "When I was presented with the first child, I found myself in a large room. Around the entire wall section of this room were see through rectangular boxes. Each box was tilted forward and resting on small tables. The boxes reminded me of the incubator that my youngest was placed in. Contained within each box was a male or female hybrid child. I was following a female Grey hybrid as she passed by the boxes. Half way through this process, I stopped at one box. I knew that within this box was one of my hybrid children, a female. She appeared to be a newborn. The female Grey reached into the box and picked up the child. She was about 10 inches long. She was thin and frail. Her appearance reminded me of the poor African children I have seen on TV who live in Third World countries and are starving to death. I did not care if she was 99% Grey and only 1% me. She was still a part of me, and my maternal instincts took over. I reached out for her. I wanted to hold her and comfort her, but the adult female wouldn't let me. She told me that I was not allowed to hold her at this time. I reached over and briefly touched the infant's soft skin, and the female Grey placed her back into the box."

Sandy was deeply touched by the experience. He continued, "Tears were flowing down my face as I felt another presence behind me. I turned and came face to face with a male hybrid. Like before, I immediately knew he was one of my hybrid children. He appeared to be in his late teens. I am six feet tall, and he was a few inches taller than me. He reached out and put his arms around me, and I placed my arms around him. He knew I was his father, and I felt his love for me. Even though he was part Grey, I could place no blame on him. Like me, he was another pawn in some grand, galactic scheme that neither of us had any control over."

Sandy was left in a fragile emotional state from that night. He fell into a deep depression. He even refused to tell his wife for fear that she would not understand his feelings for his alien hybrid children. Finally, a week later while running errands, he shared with her what had taken place. As Sandy was telling his wife what happened, he became so distraught that he had to pull his car into a parking lot. When he stopped the car, he laid his head on the steering wheel and bawled. This is the impact that these hybrid children make on those who meet them. You yearn to see them again. You wonder where they are and what they are doing. I never saw the small hybrid female again, and that has haunted me for years. I have never figured out why they did not let me see her again. It was a cruel thing to do, but they do not seem to care. It was the same for Sandy. He, too, has never seen either of his hybrid children again. Sandy continued, "The emotional pain I experienced after seeing them the first time was as great as the pain I felt not knowing if my youngest son was going to live. Thankfully, he did and is now a healthy adult. I have no idea where my hybrid children are now or if they are healthy and well. I still yearn to see them, to hold them, and to touch them just as I do my three beautiful human children."

On a personal note, I have reluctantly accepted that I, probably, will be taken until I die. If you have been taken your entire life, eventually you come to terms with the cold hard truth of this reality. Yet, I have always held out hope. Perhaps, as I get older, I will not be as useful to them and thus will not be taken as much. Since Sandy is also a "lifer," I asked his opinion. He stated, "About two years ago I began to feel as if they were letting up on me, but now I believe that the only thing that has changed is their tactics. I still have the typical abduction experiences from time to time, but in between abductions, they seem to also be playing a mind game with me. I'm not sure why, but they will show themselves to me when no abduction occurs, at least not one that I can remember. I will see them in full physical form. I once saw them peering through the glass doors of my home office."

Sandy also believes that he and his wife have been observed by the Greys during their intimate times. He recalled a couple of very unusual incidents. "We live in the country, which affords us a good bit of privacy. This allows us to leave our curtains open when we want. One night while we held each other, flashes of white light lit up our bedroom. At first I thought someone was outside taking photos. This was not the case. As I ran into the den to head outside, the den area lit up. Once outside, I saw no one. My two black Labrador dogs did not indicate that anyone or anything was around. When I returned to the bedroom, my wife informed me that the lamp on her nightstand had begun to flicker on and off. I checked the lamp, and it was working fine. Then toward the end of 2015, another very strange thing happened. One night, as my wife and I were nearing the end of our romantic evening, a five by ten foot dimensional doorway opened in front of our closed double bedroom doors. I saw nothing go in or out of the doorway. It was only there for a few seconds. However, the next morning I woke up with fifteen scratch marks of various lengths and widths on my right butt cheek."

Sandy's recent events further demonstrate that alien abductions do not stop. They may not take you as often as they have in the past. Their methods and tactics may change, but they still come. It is interesting that Sandy witnessed what appeared to be a portal open in his bedroom. I, too, have seen a portal open which I have written about in great detail. In my case, I saw the Greys along the side of my bed. I also saw through the portal and into a craft where another Grey was waiting. Many times, I have publically stated that the portals are the means by which the Greys take us. Others have described floating through a wall or through the ceiling. In essence, this is happening because their physical surroundings are no longer there and are replaced with a dimensional portal. This enables the aliens to take us quickly and undetected. I cannot reiterate this facet of the abduction process enough. I realize the concept of a portal is a difficult thing to grasp. Our understanding of quantum physics is in the preliminary stages at this point in time. That does not mean that an advanced species has not already mastered the science.

One positive thing about Sandy's case is that he has had no recall of any forced or manipulated sexual interludes for about ten years. Did they get all they needed from him? Do they stop certain procedures when an abductee reaches a certain age? Is it different for each person? In time, I will find my answers. Sandy did state that they continue to extract sperm from him using a hypodermic needle device. The pain afterward is not as severe as it once was. He feels that they are now using a type of numbing agent on the area before the extraction. That is one of the paradoxes about the Greys. Although they show no signs of real emotions like love, kindness or compassion, they will do things to help their captive subjects. Placing a numbing agent on Sandy's testicles is a prime example.

I asked Sandy for any final thoughts. "I know that I am alien abductee," he simply stated. "I have been having abduction experiences since the age of five. I know that they are ongoing. I do not like my abductions because of the pain and confusion I have had to endure, not just from the aliens but from humans as well. The pain has been physical, mental, spiritual, and emotional." Sandy continued, "It is hard enough for humans to survive the human reality, but it is much more difficult to survive the alien reality as well. I have learned that I am much stronger than I thought. These experiences have shaped who I have become. We all know that our species loves a good mystery, and we, abductees, are part of one of the biggest and most important mysteries of all time." It is because of people like Sandy and other Experiencers that we are closer to solving this elusive mystery. When it comes to the subject of alien abductions, cognitive dissonance is rampant. Ignoring, denying, or hiding from the truth does not eliminate the truth. It still remains whether you accept it or not. Someday this mystery will be solved. The question will then be—where do we go from here?

Chapter 8

Recollection

"You look so familiar. Haven't we met before?" It sounds like a bad pickup line, but we have probably all had someone ask us this question. Perhaps, you have seen someone who looked hauntingly familiar, but you could not remember where you might have met him or her. These kind of confusing occurrences happen to all of us at one time or another. For the alien abductee, the dynamic changes when this question is asked. There is always the possibility that this person does not remember you from a party, a class, work or a myriad of other places; they remember you from an alien craft. Sometimes, they are so convinced they have seen you during an abduction event that they feel strongly compelled to tell you. This has happened to me on more than one occasion. Once while setting up my laptop to give a talk in Nashville, Tennessee, a man came up to me and blurted out, "I saw you. I saw you on a craft." I was a bit taken aback by his assertiveness. I looked up from my computer. Before I could respond, he asked me to look closely at him. "Do you remember me?" he asked me. "I know you were there. You looked right at me. We didn't speak, but I know it was you," he adamantly declared. I looked at him for a few seconds. "I'm sorry sir, but I don't remember seeing you on a craft," I replied. He kept shaking his head as if in shock that I did not remember him.

I do not mean to imply that this man did not recognize me from an abduction incident. It is certainly within the realm of possibility. We all remember different things. No one remembers every abduction event. The same thing happened to me while giving another talk in

Lebanon, Tennessee one night. While standing in front of the room giving my presentation, my attention kept being drawn to a woman sitting in the far back corner of the room. I kept glancing at her. Just like the man who had come up to me, I was convinced I had seen this woman during an abduction event. At the end of my presentation, I tried my best to make my way back to her and introduce myself but got diverted. As was often the case, people came up wanting to meet me and ask more questions. After a few minutes, I looked up, and she was gone. I was very disappointed that I never got the chance to speak to her. I was convinced that she was the one I had seen. I would have been just as bold as the man who spoke up to me. I would have directly asked her if she remembered me.

I spoke to a friend of mine before I left that night. He knew several of the people who had attended my presentation. I told him about the woman who seemed so familiar. When I mentioned where she was sitting, he said that he knew her. I was relieved to find out I might still have a chance to meet her. My friend called her and set up a meeting. A couple of weeks later, I did get to meet this woman. She was very nice and had a good personality. I told her about the memory I had of seeing her. She did not remember seeing me or the event I described to her. I did learn, however, that she had been having alien abduction experiences since she was a child. To this day, I am positive it was her. Just because she does not remember seeing me, does not mean that it did not happen. When another abductee tells me they have seen me during an abduction event, I always remain open to the very real possibility that they did.

This was exactly how I met Susan. She saw a photo of me and was convinced that she had seen me on a craft and had interacted with me as well. She was so convinced that she found me on Facebook and reached out to me. I listened to her account; it did not sound familiar to me. Even though I did not remember the event Susan related to me, I was intrigued enough to learn more about her and her abduction experiences. After doing so, I asked Susan if she would be willing to share some of her experiences in this book. She agreed as long as her identity was not revealed. I assured her that she would remain anonymous. I pray that the day will come when the thousands of individuals, having alien encounters around the world, will be able to speak freely about them without fear of the resulting ramifications. For now, I applaud the courage of those who, at least, are willing to share their own personal accounts.

Susan recounted the time when she thought she saw me on an alien craft. "I was home alone and cleaning the house. All of a sudden, I was on a ship. I was walking around the ship freely, and I saw people lying on tables. There was a man strapped to a table who was yelling. There was a girl there who couldn't have been more than 13 or 14 years old. She was hysterical and screaming. The aliens saw me and took me over to the man on the table and asked me if I could make him stop yelling. I patted the man on the shoulder and told him, 'You have to be calm. They will ask you questions. They won't be so scary, and they will talk to you.' I tried to tell the young girl that too. I saw that they were doing reproductive things to her. I was so angry about that. I told the Greys how wrong it was; she was too young." Susan continued, "When I saw a photo of you and found out that you were an abductee, I said, 'Oh my God! He looks just like the man that I saw. This is the man that I saw." Susan concluded her account by saying, "On that particular day, the aliens wanted me to comfort the other humans. I wasn't doing a very good job, but I tried. All of a sudden, I was back in my kitchen, and I noticed that I had an hour of missing time."

Susan had experienced several incidents like this. Each time, the Greys had asked her to try and calm people, to make them stop crying, or make them less afraid. She said she obeyed their commands even though she was not always successful in achieving what they wanted. Interestingly, most of these abductions, in which she was asked to calm people, happened during the day. They were also of shorter duration. Although most abductions happen during the night, they can and do take place during the day also. Because of the dimensional aspects of this phenomenon, one has to consider that the aliens have the ability to alter the space/time continuum. What may seem like an hour of missing time to someone like Susan may, in reality, be several hours or more in "their" time. Perhaps we are gone for a much longer duration than we think. Maybe this explains why so many abductees feel extreme exhaustion after an abduction event. Have we been awake for an extended period of time? Many of us have noticed that our hair and fingernails seem to grow faster than normal. Is this due to the actual time we are gone and not the few hours we think we have been gone?

When Susan first told me this story, something occurred to me. Since the Greys have done both mental and physical experiments on their subjects, I suggested that these incidents, in which she was asked to calm others, might have been a mental experiment or mind game. It was something that she had not considered, but she agreed that could have been the case. Maybe at some point, she had seen me on a craft. Maybe she had also seen the young girl and the other humans who were strapped to tables during other abduction experiences. The Greys could have simply pulled the memories of me and the other humans from Susan's subconscious mind and created the scenario of everyone being in distress. They could have been testing her. They would then monitor her emotional reactions to the other humans. They would see if she demonstrated kindness and compassion to the others; they would see if she easily obeyed or resisted if given her freedom. This is a probable scenario, and most likely what happened.

From my experience with the Greys, I have never been strapped to a table. The Greys have such mind control capabilities that they have no need to strap anyone down to keep them in place. In addition, Susan noticed the reproductive procedure being performed on the young girl. She noted how upset she became when witnessing what was being done to this girl. This would be the type of thing that the Greys would do to illicit a response from someone. They would then monitor that response to see how the individual was affected psychologically. I found this situation odd and not typical of their usual behavior. Considering everything, I believe it may have been another mind game. Of course, I do not know for sure, and I doubt Susan does either. It does, however, fall right in line with normal Grey behavior.

Like many other abductees, Susan's first experiences with the Greys began around the age of five. She is now middle age, and her experiences have continued. Susan is a "lifer." She recalled her first incidents, "I was hypervigilant as a child. I still am to this day. I would lay awake at night with my eyes open, and I would watch the room. On more than one occasion, I saw three little faces reach for me from the foot of my bed. I looked at them. They were the size of children, around four feet tall. I would see them just staring at me. I didn't feel particularly threatened by them. It was just scary. I would scream for my parents. My Dad would come running in, but, by the time he got to my room, they would be gone. Because they were about my size, I thought that they were some kind of strange, little playmates." The Greys made no attempt to erase the memories of their visits to Susan's room. However, since she does not remember ever being on a craft or being taken during those early years, I suspect that they did suppress some of her memories.

These mysterious visitations continued for Susan. After a while she quit screaming for her Dad. She realized that he was never going to see them since they always disappeared before he arrived. When Susan started school, she made the mistake of telling the other kids about her strange looking friends who would visit her at night. She did so innocently, but she soon found herself teased and mocked so severely that she shut down. Her memories about her little visitors stopped and did not surface again until the 1990's. Unfortunately, being teased and mocked is all too real for Experiencers, regardless of their age.

As she matured, Susan noticed that she had psychic abilities. As I previously mentioned, this is a common trait among Experiencers. Susan began to have OBEs (Out of body experiences). They started when she was young, and, at first, they would happen spontaneously. Over the years, Susan learned to control them. In the 1990's, the abductions started again, and they came with a vengeance. As her abductions increased, she noticed that her psychic abilities increased as well. She would have as many as three OBEs a day. Susan elaborated, "I would lie down, and I would go out of my body. It was like I was being directed where to go. I showed up at many accident scenes, earthquakes, plane crashes, and all kinds of tragic events. At first, I could feel someone pulling me by the hand and taking me to these places. I could hear someone instructing me to watch from above and see what was happening. I would see people lying on the ground or trapped inside a car. I couldn't tell if the person was alive or dead. I was told to look into their chest, so I started doing that. The first time I did, I saw a small flickering light right in the middle of the person's chest. I was told that, when I saw that light, the body was still viable. This went on for over a year. It was like I was in an apprentice training program.

One time, I was taken to a restaurant. It was a Friday night, and I was standing in the middle of this busy restaurant. The woman who was my guide said, 'Look around. Who are you here for? Why did we bring you here?' I looked around the whole room, and I had no idea. She told me to look for something that was out of order, so I looked for the longest time. The only thing that seemed strange was this couple sitting at a table. They had been there longer than anyone else, and they hadn't been waited on. They were getting upset that they were not getting any service. I told my guide that I felt it was them. My guide confirmed that I was right and nudged me to go over and interact with them. I went over to their table, but I didn't know what to say to them. By that time, I knew what had happened to them. I didn't really know how to break the news to them, so I just stood by their table.

Finally, I asked them if anything about the situation seemed weird to them. They said that nothing seemed weird. They were just having trouble getting waited on because the restaurant was very busy. They asked me to go away, but I just stood there. I knew they were ghosts; they were dead. I leaned over the table, got right in their faces, and shouted, 'boo' loudly. It startled them, and they asked me why I did that. I explained to them what had happened. I told them they were never going to be waited on because no one could see them but me. They got really upset and told me to leave; they insisted they were fine. I told them they had been in a car wreck on the way to the restaurant. I described the accident; it was a head on collision, and they both had died instantly. I explained to them that the accident had happened so fast that they just continued on to the restaurant for date night. They were shocked and scared when I told them this. They became very confused as they remembered the accident. They asked me what they were supposed to do. I told them to keep going, and someone would find them and lead them to where they were supposed to go. I walked back over to my guide and asked her how I did. She said, 'Everything was fine. You did well; except, you don't say boo to people who have died.'"

I am proud of Susan. She has taken her ability, which most likely stemmed from her abduction experiences, and turned it into something positive. It is imperative that anyone who has endured these abductions not become a victim. Empower yourself in your everyday existence. This is what Susan did. Instead of ignoring her OBEs or trying to stop them from happening, she learned to control them and began to use her ability to help others. Susan's guide revealed to her the daunting task of helping these lost, confused souls, and she embraced this responsibility of helping them make their transition to the other side. What a beautiful, compassionate act.

Many experiencers have reported disruptions of electrical equipment in their presence. They have reported things like televisions shutting on and off or switching channels, watches not keeping proper time, and even lights blowing when they are near. I have personally experienced most of these anomalies myself, and some were quite extreme. Once, I was walking down a street at night and saw several street lights go out as soon as I walked under them. I attribute these unusual incidents to the increased energy one acquires when passing through the dimensional portals of the aliens. While talking to Susan, I learned that she, too, has experienced these strange electrical occurrences. She also told me about another very odd thing that has happened to her.

"I bend metal or rather metal bends on me," Susan proclaimed. "I used to carry a hammer with me in my car. I would get out of the car and go in somewhere. By the time I was ready to leave, my keys would be bent over like arthritic fingers. I would have to lay them on the sidewalk and hammer them back into shape, so I could get the car key into the ignition. This went on for almost five years. When it first started, my husband accused me of playing with the keys and inadvertently bending them. I handed him the keys and told him to bend one. He couldn't move it. He realized then that something strange was happening. One time, it happened at a MUFON meeting. I was sitting at one of their support group meetings and noticed that my car keys had bent during the meeting. They were fine when I walked in. I showed them to people in the support group, and MUFON took pictures. They weren't bent as drastically as they had been at other times, but they were still bent."

Susan continued, "My wedding ring was the first thing to bend on me. It was a little 14 carat gold band. I woke up one morning, and my finger was swollen to the point that it was turning blue. I could not get the ring off. I went into the bathroom to soap up my finger. I still could not remove my ring. Finally, with my husband's help, the ring came off and went flying into the sink. When we picked it up, it was in the shape of a squashed doughnut. I never had it bent back. I wear it on a gold chain now." Susan reported that other jewelry would bend on her also, especially earrings. She had a pair of earrings that her brother had given her as a gift. She loved them, but they too would bend when worn. Various household objects did as well. Eating utensils would bend as she was using them. One time, she noticed indentation marks where her fingers had been holding a metal drinking cup. Her kids were so freaked out by it that they refused to use it, so she eventually threw it out.

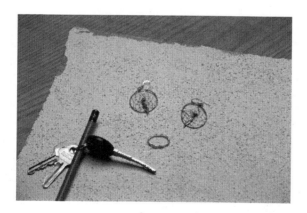

Some of Susan's objects that bent

In March of 1994, Susan became fully aware of her abductions. Either she or the Greys had blocked her early childhood memories of being taken. She had always felt an inner knowing that something had been going on her entire life even though she had no memories. Everything changed that night in March. Her instincts were validated by an encounter with alien visitors. Susan recalled the terrifying incident, "My husband and I had just gone to bed when we heard dogs barking. We had an outside dog at the time, and my husband went outside to check on our dog. He decided to put our dog in his work van to protect him from the pack of dogs that was running around the neighborhood. He said that he was going to lie on the couch, and if those dogs came back, he was going to fire a shot over their heads to scare them off. I couldn't go to sleep. I was just lying there waiting on him. I looked at the clock, and it was around 12:30. I was annoyed that he hadn't come back to bed. After several minutes, I turned over to look at the clock again. As I did, the room filled with a brilliant blue light. It was like a neon black light had engulfed the room."

"At that moment, I remembered all the stuff that had happened to me in my life. I was like, 'Oh my God, Oh my God! Here it is again!' Susan exclaimed. Part of her was absolutely terrified while another part felt calm. She quickly began to have an inner dialogue with herself trying to rationalize what was happening. "I told myself that I was safe because all the doors and windows were locked. Then I realized that they don't enter through doors and windows. The frightened part of me began to pray, but the calm part of me knew that prayer wouldn't stop this from happening." Susan continued, "I screamed as loud as I could. Somebody was going to hear me either my husband or the neighbors. Somebody was going to wake up. When I did, it was like I screamed into a vacuum, and no one heard me. I finally gave up and accepted that this was going to happen. I remembered thinking to myself that I didn't want to remember it, and I didn't want to see their faces. I was already on my side from turning over to look at the clock, so I turned over on my stomach and buried my face in my pillow. As I did, I felt the covers being pulled back, and I felt someone grab me by my ankles and start pulling me over the little footboard of the bed. I was holding on to the pillow for dear life. I kept thinking, 'I don't want to see their faces, but for some reason, I had to look."

Susan recalled the shock of what she saw, "I lifted up my head, and I looked over my right shoulder. There, at the foot of the bed, stood the same three little guys that used to come in my room when I was a child. In the blue light, their skin looked powdery white. I remember exactly what they looked like." Susan declared. "I've only seen a couple of renderings that I can say, with certainty, looked like them. They had tiny ears on the side of their head. Their eyes were more round than elongated, and they were big, too big. They weren't like the typical eyes we associate with the Greys." Susan continued, "They had tiny noses and small mouths. Their faces were rounder than the typical Grey also. They were wearing loose cloaks with a loose fitting hood. In the blue light, the cloaks looked like an indigo blue color. I couldn't look anymore, so I put my face back into my pillow. They just kept pulling me off the bed. The next thing I knew, I was being tucked back into bed. The blue light was still on. Then all of a sudden, it was gone. I rose up to look at the clock, and it was almost 4:30. My husband was still not in bed. Four hours of time was gone in an instant."

After that event, Susan's life became an emotional roller coaster. She had come to the realization that she was an alien abductee. Oddly enough, the first thing she felt was euphoria. "For three days after that night, I felt absolute euphoria. I was convinced that the experience was very beautiful." Susan explained. "Then after three days, I went into a very deep depression with extreme anxiety. I was terrified to go anywhere, even in the daytime. I didn't drive for six months, and I would not go outside by myself at night." Susan's erratic emotions demonstrate the trauma that is often induced by an alien abduction incident. Fear takes over and dictates your life. You are constantly on edge; your mind is filled with the fear that they will return. You know in your heart that it is not really a question of "if" but "when."

In April of that same year, Susan's fear became a reality; the unwanted visitors returned. This time was different. They did not come for her. It was a much worse scenario. They came for her son, and she could do nothing to stop it. Susan recalled that horrifying night, "I was lying in bed one night, and I saw the blue light again. This time it wasn't in my room; it was in one of my children's rooms. All I could do was raise up on my elbows, and that was it. I could go no farther. It was like something was holding me there. I was so angry that I couldn't go into the room where my youngest son was sleeping. Two years before, he had told us that something had happened in his room. He was 12 years old then. At that time, my memory hadn't come back with all this stuff, and I was trying to find a logical explanation. My son was very angry with us. He even drew what he saw, which has since disappeared from our house. He told us aliens were in his room, and one of them was poking him with a little ball of light. He said it looked like a pool stick with a ball of light on it. He said there was a man that looked like he was on fire standing outside his window. I asked him what he meant, and he said that the man had so much light coming off of him that he had to be on fire. He got angry with my husband and me because we couldn't understand what was happening to him. Looking back now, I understand how frustrating it must have been for him."

Susan soon discovered that "they" weren't just interested in her younger son; they were interested in both of her children. She continued, "Two nights later, I saw the same blue light enter my older son's room. Once again, the aliens immobilized me, and I was unable to move. Neither of my sons said anything, but they were acting strangely. I sat them down one afternoon and I thought, 'do I tell them, or do I not tell them?' I decided to tell them what had happened to me and see what kind of response I got from them. They told me they believed me, but they did not want to talk about it. Eventually, I found out that both of my sons remembered being taken by the Greys. One day my oldest son told me that he had been taken the previous night. He was confused and upset. He said, 'Mama they were here last night. They took me to this place. There were babies floating in Coke bottles.' That's how he described it. I reassured him that it wasn't Coke bottles and that the babies weren't dead. I told him that they were keeping the babies alive in the fluid just like in a mother's womb. I was also shown the babies. The first time I saw them, I thought the babies were dead and were being preserved in formaldehyde. I wanted to throw up! Then I realized that they were alive." Susan now knew that the Greys were also taking both of her sons. Years later at a family reunion, she learned the shocking truth about other family members.

She found out that her father and other members on his side of the family had been taken for years. This is not uncommon, for the Greys tend to stay with the same family line for generations.

Susan had seen the Tall Greys, the small Greys, and the small variation Greys with rounded eyes that she described earlier. Like so many other abductees, she has been subjected to a myriad of different procedures and experiments. I asked Susan about some of the procedures done to her by the Greys. "One time they took me, and I was lying on a table. The small Greys took a small clear tube device and inserted it into the right side of my abdomen. It was very painful," She said. "Even though I was in pain, I tried to remain calm. I had learned that if I remained calm and didn't freak out, they would communicate with me. I asked the one who had inserted the tube what he was doing. He replied telepathically that they were removing DNA." She continued, "They removed the tube, placed it on a metal tray, and left the room with it. A few minutes later, they returned with another tube and inserted that tube into my abdomen. I asked again, 'what are you doing now?' They told me that they were replacing DNA. I was very confused, but for some reason, I didn't ask them why."

I find it odd that these creatures will perform painful, invasive procedures without showing the slightest bit of compassion, yet they will often take the time to explain what they are doing. Sometimes they will honor your request. This was the case with me when I asked the Tall Grey to remove the implant in my nasal passage due to chronic nosebleeds. I mentioned this to Susan and asked if she or either of her sons had been implanted. She replied, "My son suffered from severe nosebleeds. I took him to the doctor several times, but they weren't able to help. Finally I took him to an Ear, Nose, and Throat specialist. The doctor was examining him and said, 'Oh, this is odd. He's nicked an artery.' I asked the doctor how that was even possible. He did not answer. He told me that he was going to cauterize it which helped for a while, but eventually the nosebleeds returned." Susan then recalled her own experience with what seemed to be an implant, "I was sitting in a theatre one day. I'm not sure how to explain it, but I felt something come loose in my head and roll down the back of my throat into my mouth. I spit it out into my hand. It looked like a small BB. I was so freaked out. I thought, 'I don't want this; I don't want this,' so I threw it. I was so upset that I got up and left the theatre. I immediately called my friend from MUFON and told her what had happened. She said it sounded like an implant had come loose. She was very disappointed that I had gotten scared and threw the object in the theatre."

Like so many other Experiencers, Susan was also shown images of catastrophic earth events by the Greys. I was shown various scenes of war, extreme poverty, floods, fires, and nuclear bomb explosions. Once I asked the Tall Grey why he was showing this to me. Everything they showed me had already happened on Earth. I got the impression that they wanted to measure my emotional response to this stimulus. Perhaps, it was a warning or sorts. I told the Tall Grey that I knew they would not let us destroy the planet; they would stop us. He seemed satisfied with my answer, and we left the screen with the images. Susan felt much the same as I did about the images she was shown. She told the Tall Grey to not blame all humans for the actions of a few; most of us were worth saving. She begged him to not let us destroy the earth. In essence, she asked the aliens for help, whether or not her pleas fell on deaf ears remains to be seen.

That was not the only time the Greys showed Susan images. "One night they projected a light beam in front of me. In it, there were images of a newborn baby with dark hair. I saw about five or six different babies. I saw the Greys stretching a baby out and measuring it in a strange way. It was not the way we measure newborn babies. They stretched the foot down so the toes were pointed as far as they could point. Then they raised the arms above the head. They measured from the tips of the fingers to the end of where the toes pointed. They also measured the circumference of the head and a few other body measurements." Susan continued, "I was looking at the baby they were examining. There was a female or, possibly, a hybrid with me. I asked, 'Is that me?' She acknowledged that it was me when I was a newborn. I was shocked. I then asked for confirmation, 'So this has been going on since I was a newborn?' She said, 'Yes, do you feel like you are part of the family?' I said all humans are part of a family. We have parents, children, pets, and other relatives. She told me that was not what she meant. She said I was a part of a different kind of family. At the time, I did not understand what she meant. I do now."

The most insidious and invasive act of the Greys is the removal of a fetus from a human female. The horror of that despicable deed often induces more trauma than any other alien abduction experience. Such was the case with Susan. She could not talk about it. She would only acknowledge the fact that, over the years, she had had several fetuses removed by the Greys. Susan was, however, able to talk about the hybrid children who were presented to her by her alien captors. She related the encounter, "I was introduced to four hybrid children, all at the same time. I was told they were mine. It's strange, but when I saw the children, I felt compelled to name them. I told the Greys that they had to have names. There was one little girl maybe about five or six years old. She had red hair. I named her Bridget. There was another slightly older girl with brown hair. I decided to call her Stephanie. There was a little boy that was younger than the two females. He also had brown hair. I named him Samuel. The fourth hybrid child was an infant that they placed in my arms. He was also a male, and I named him Joseph. I'm not sure why I chose the names that I did. They were just the first names that popped into my head."

Susan continued, "The Greys asked me if I thought the children could pass for humans if placed on earth. The one that looked the most human was the little red haired girl. The others were very feral. I told the Greys that the other three looked human, but they would not blend in well. I pointed to the female with the red hair and told them that she was the only one who could go unnoticed in our society. She seemed excited that I was there and was very affectionate. She was the only child that interacted with me. She knew that I was her mother, and I wanted to bring her back with me. They told me that I couldn't have her. I never saw her again. To this day, I keep hoping that someday I'll hear a knock on my door, and I'll see a woman with red hair. She'll say, 'Hi Mom. I'm Bridget.'

Susan accepts that she is a "lifer." She knows that the extra-terrestrial visitors will not stop coming for her. In the fall of 2016, she experienced something different. A visitor showed up, but it was not the Greys. Susan recalled the unusual encounter, "I was lying in bed trying to go to sleep. I still have a difficult time going to sleep. Sometimes it will be 2 or 3 o'clock in the morning before I finally fall asleep. This time it was about midnight. I saw this misty blue form start to appear beside the bed. It had a humanoid shape, but it was not completely humanoid. I was not afraid; I was more in awe than anything. I kept trying to figure out what it was. I watched for a couple of minutes, and then it dissipated and was gone. The next night, I was lying in bed. I was trying so hard to go to sleep, and I just couldn't. I opened my eyes and was shocked to see a person standing beside the bed. The being had blue skin and no hair. It looked somewhat humanoid, but there were differences. The skull was different in the back, and there were other slight differences. It was more humanoid than alien looking; it was solid, as solid as you and me."

Susan recalled what happened next, "It was standing there looking down at me. Somehow, when I looked into its eyes, I knew that I wasn't in any danger. In fact, it was quite the opposite. I felt very safe for some reason. It reached its hands out with palms down and placed both hands about two feet above my body and held them there. It then closed its eyes, as if, in some kind of meditative state; it stayed there for a few minutes. Then it removed its hands and instantly disappeared. I assumed that it was giving me some kind of healing as I was not in a good place mentally at the time." Was the mysterious visitor that came to Susan that night an extraterrestrial healer? Was he an ethereal being looking after her and giving her much needed inner strength? Personally, I find comfort knowing that benevolent beings are out there and willing to help the victims of alien abduction. Like Susan, many of us, who remember our experiences, find that recollection is not always kind.

Chapter 9

It's My Life

Or is it? Anyone who has spent his entire life being taken by alien visitors begins to lose a sense of self. It is an inevitable psychological consequence of being taken against your will and being forced to relinquish all control of your mind and body. Eventually, you stop trying to resist as you realize its futility. You accept that both intrusive and painful things will be done to your body. Even if you attempt to fight back, you realize you are unable. Your screams of both pain and anger are silenced, never to escape the confines of your mind. When the alien experiences first begin, fear is the primary emotion that surfaces. Over time, fear subsides and anger takes its place. You soon realize that neither fear nor anger will serve you. If anything, they make matters worse. I learned a long time ago that cooperation was a key component in getting through the ordeal of an abduction event. Now when I am taken, I focus on one integral thing – survival. That is really all that matters. I have learned to let go of everything else. I just want to survive, whatever it is that I am subjected to, and make it home once more.

It has taken a lot of effort and time, but, for the most part, my fear of the Greys has substantially diminished. I do my best to face my experiences with resolve and strength. Do I want them to stop? Absolutely! Do I believe that they will stop? Absolutely not! That is a sobering thought, but one that every abductee has to face and accept if he/she is to begin the healing process. In the end, I am left with only two fears in regards to what has happened to me. One is that the aliens will take someone else from my family. Knowing that they, especially the Greys, stay with a particular DNA line is a frightening thought. I would not wish what has happened to me on anyone and certainly not a loved one. This is a scenario that has a high probability of taking place. It may already be happening, and my family member has not yet had any memories of the events surface. I only have one child, a daughter. When she was four years old, she told me about the little men that came in her room. When she told me that, I was instantly overwhelmed with despair. The feeling of helplessness in this situation is indescribable. This is one fear I cannot conquer. I simply do my best to live with it.

The second fear I live with on a daily basis is one that is not often addressed in the UFO community. It has to do with implants. It is not a fear of having an implant placed in my body. One of the first memories that many abductees have is implant placement. Some of the most commonly reported locations for implants are insertions through a nostril near the optic nerve, areas directly behind the ear, and in the back of the head near the medulla oblongata. Insertions in areas near the spine and other parts of the body have also been reported. I have written about the memory of my nasal implant and the chronic nosebleeds it caused me to have; this continued for years. The doctors could never find a medical reason for the nosebleeds or any way to make me stop having them. They could only offer suggestions as to what to do once I had one. My chronic nosebleeds only stopped after I actually asked the Greys to remove the implant in my nasal cavity and move it somewhere else. Surprisingly enough, they obliged my request. I have no memory of when and where it was moved. However, soon after that request, I did notice a strange new bump behind my left ear that is still there to this day. I cannot say with any degree of certainty whether or not the odd bump is indeed an alien implant. I only know that the bump appeared soon after my request for them to remove the implant. I am certain that they would keep an implant in me.

I believe that there are different size implants. An individual can be implanted with more than one implant device, with each device performing a different function. I am positive that nano technology is being used by every advanced alien species. It is only logical to assume that they would utilize that technology with implants. The size of an implant can vary depending on its use and where it is placed in the body of the receiver. Whatever the case, I think it is generally accepted that human abductees are treated like specimens and implanted with some kind of device. To some, it is likened to how we brand cattle, simply a way to assist in indentifying the subject. Still others believe that the alien implants are a sophisticated tracking device. This hypothesis is offered as a way to explain how experiencers are found and taken no matter where they are located. I believe that both ideas are correct. Yes, the implants are used to identify the subject, and yes, it is definitely used to track and locate the subject. I also believe that there may be a more sinister use of the implants. That brings me back to my second remaining fear. It is not the implant itself that I fear or the process of being implanted. It is the fear that the implant may be used to control the thoughts and, thus, the actions of those in whom it is placed.

I went for decades knowing that I was implanted and believing that it was nothing more than a tracking device. I have moved numerous times, and no matter where I moved, the abductions persisted. The implants had to be tracking me. What better way to find those they have taken than to place a tracking device in them? I used to marvel at the technology behind that before our own modern GPS and tracking systems were developed. Of course, like many other recent technological advances, I believe that we were given that technology by the aliens. Not given in the sense that it was freely given but rather a trade off of sorts; the governments look the other way while their citizens are abducted. They then reap the benefits of advanced technology. Once the initial technology is revealed, it is copied and spread throughout the world.

The science behind alien implants is no different. Reports are being released revealing just how advanced we have become in regards to nano technology and neuroscience. It is almost incomprehensible to even imagine the magnitude of what could happen to our world should an implant be developed combining these two sciences. It would be small. It could be injected, travel through the bloodstream to the brain, attach to the brain, and trigger neurons in the brain that could control every thought. A nanometer is one millionth of a millimeter. It is so small that it can only be seen with a microscope. In essence, it would be like having a microscopic computer inserted in your brain. The problem is that you would not control the computer. If humans are developing this kind of technology, then be assured that an advanced alien species has already been using it for a very long time. It is possible that the implant is what enables the aliens to easily communicate telepathically with humans. I believe that these implants are able to measure syntax sensory information which allows the aliens to see and hear what the implanted person is seeing and hearing. Even more alarming, the aliens can read and monitor your thoughts and even maintain a direct conversation with your mind. The abductee may have thoughts that seem like his own, but in reality, the thoughts are placed there by the aliens. This is the rationale behind my second fear.

Like most people, I have begun to look back at things in my life more often. There are fond memories that bring a smile to my face. There are the sad memories that bring back a sense of loss as I remember friends and loved ones who have made the transition to the other side. I have looked back at my successes and also my failures. Of course, regret will occasionally rear its ugly head. Like most people, I have regrets. There are always things from the past that you wish you had done differently. One tends to have a much different perspective when looking back than when the event is taking place. I have often looked back at certain events and felt like I was watching myself in a movie, but I did not write the script. I am the type of person who usually takes my time when making a decision, yet there have been times throughout my life that I felt compelled to make a decision that was completely out of character. I did things knowing they were not right for me but did them anyway with no explanation as to why. Maybe this happens to everyone. My life has never been normal, so I have no way of knowing if this is normal behavior. I do know what it feels like to be controlled, and I do know there have been times in my everyday life that it felt like I was being controlled.

Are certain events in my life and other abductees happening because the Greys want them to happen? Do they put you in situations to monitor you for their own particular agenda? They are keenly interested in human emotions. It would seem logical that not all of their experiments would be done on board a craft or at some hidden base. By controlling their subject through implants, they could set up scenarios and events that are real life situations and not an experiment based solely on what they have pulled from the subject's subconscious. It is possible that the alien puppet masters bring certain individuals together in relationships and conversely tear them apart. Author Eve Lorgen, who has a Master's degree in counseling psychology, has written an entire book on the subject. She coined the term the "love bite" which is also the name of her book. Lorgen believes, like I do, that aliens are interfering in human relationships. Understanding the motives behind this interference is one of the most overlooked components to uncovering the truth behind their agenda.

Lorgen describes the love bite as "a kind of psychic rape" whereby the victim is abducted and manipulated into bonding with a targeted love partner chosen by the alien beings. The effects of the love bite can range from simple break-ups in platonic relationships to violent divorces and from "puppy love to sudden urges to marry a complete stranger." More specifically, she describes the love bite as "the interference in human erotic and romantic relationships." As you might imagine, this kind of alien interference goes way beyond just a physical abduction and leaves behind deep emotional scars. I have often stated that the emotional aspects of the abduction experience are the most painful and most difficult to overcome. Not only does the abductee have to cope with the ordeal of being taken against his will, subjected to various invasive physical examinations and experiments, but he/she also has to live with the possibility that these strange creatures have the ability to control one's everyday life, including romantic relationships. Trust becomes a serious issue because of this. Are your feelings real, or are you being controlled and manipulated by an unseen but ever present force? You begin to question everything about any relationship, unable to discern the reality of your feelings or the other person's true feelings. The questions are many. Did the aliens bring this person into your life and, if so, why? Is it for your benefit, the aliens, or the other party? Will it last, or will the aliens cause it to end once their mission is completed?

Critics of Eve Lorgen's love bite hypothesis claim that everyone has relationship problems, and she is merely blaming aliens for a human problem. Lorgen answers her critics explaining that her research indicates that abductees represent a separate modality that fit a certain profile. The number of abductees that meet the criteria of a love bite goes way beyond the percentage of the general population. It is sobering to think that our alien captors may be doing this regardless of motive or reason. To me, it is a reprehensible act. If they are indeed monitoring my thoughts, I hope they have learned how I feel about it. I am sure that even the emotions I emit concerning it interests them. There is no way to prove if the implants are being used in a nefarious manner. However, researchers such as Eve Lorgen and others present some compelling evidence; countless abductees and Experiencers also agree with the findings. To me, it is a logical extension of the modus operandi of the Greys and most likely any other species, alien or human, they are working with. Their normal behavior and treatment of the hapless person taken is far from altruistic. Over and over, "they" exert their will on the humans they take during the abduction event. They clearly demonstrate powerful telepathic abilities. Are these supreme telepathic powers due to their advanced intellect or is the real power in the technology they use, i.e. implants?

To venture closer to that elusive answer, we must first explore the wide range of psychic abilities associated with telepathy. Most people are familiar with the term telepathy but do not realize that it describes a wide range of abilities such as reading, projecting, and manipulating thoughts. Parapsychology describes four basic forms of telepathy.

- **Latent telepathy**, formerly known as deferred telepathy, is described as the transfer of information with an observable time-lag between transmission and reception.

- **Retrocognitive, precognitive and intuitive telepathy** is described as being the transfer of information about past, present or future information to another individual.

- **Emotive telepathy**, also known as remoter influence or emotional transfer, is the process of transferring kinesthetic sensations through altered states.

- **Superconscious telepathy** involves tapping into the superconscious to access the collective wisdom of the human species for knowledge.

In science fiction, these telepathic abilities are taken to more extreme levels. Most of us have watched Sci-fi movies where either super heroes or an alien species possess some kind of supreme telepathic ability. Telepathic abilities, such as the following, are commonly used by the Greys.

- **Binding**: The ability to restrict the movement of others via the mind.

- **Illusion Manipulation:** The ability to manipulate what others perceive. Someone may see things that are not present or not see things that are.

- **Knowledge Projection:** The ability to project knowledge onto another mind.

- **Memory Reading:** The ability to read the target's memories.

- **Mind Image:** The ability to project your own or any other image into the mind of another.

- **Thought Manipulation:** The ability to control the thoughts of others.

- **Omnilingualism:** The ability to intuitively understand all languages.

- **Mental Inducement:** The ability to place the target's mind into the desired state.

- **Psychic Inhibitors:** The placing of inhibitors in the mind of another in order to limit that individual's capabilities.

Those who have a myopic view of psychic phenomena dismiss these abilities as mere science fiction and not science fact. Of course, I assume that their views on the subject would only pertain to human psychic abilities and not alien ones. If psychic abilities did not exist in humans, the CIA and other governments around the world would not be so interested in the subject. They fully understand the power it holds and harnessing that power would be a prime directive for them. In his book, *Mind Controllers* author Armen Victorian discusses the formation of the CIA and its immediate interest in mind control, "Under the provisions of the National Security Act of 1947, the CIA was established. One of the main areas investigated by the CIA was mind control. The program was motivated by Soviet, Chinese and North Korean use of mind control techniques. The CIA originated its first program in 1950 under the name BLUEBIRD. MKULTRA officially began in 1953. In 1973, tipped off about forthcoming investigations, CIA director Richard Helms ordered the destruction of any MKULTRA records. The Senate Intelligence Committee did find some records during its investigation in 1976. Senator Frank Church, who led the congressional investigation of the CIA's unlawful actions, said that the agency was 'a rogue elephant' operating above the law as it plotted assassinations, illegally spied on thousands of Americans, and even drugged citizens in its effort to develop new weapons for its covert arsenal. In 1977, through a Freedom of Information Act request, 16,000 pages of mind control documents were found as part of the Agency's financial history. This is how this information has been pieced together."

Eventually the CIA's secret MKULTRA project grew and expanded into various branches of research and experimentation. One of the main objectives was the development of the ability to control the actions of an individual and to induce total and complete amnesia in the subject, no matter the conditions or circumstances of the event. They also sought to completely control a subject's personality and to be able to quickly instigate full mind control of an individual. Does this sound familiar? It does to me. Mankind's secret programs around the world all stem from one simple truth. Mind control is the ultimate weapon. When one has the capability to control the thoughts and actions of another, he possesses supreme power. What good does a weapon serve if the mind of the operator of that weapon can be controlled? What purpose does a soldier serve if, through mind control, he is told to disobey orders? The implications of mind control do not stop there. Consider the possibility of a world leader being manipulated by mind control. This is a scary thought. Entire populations could theoretically be controlled turning mankind into slaves to be used for whatever agenda the controllers desired.

The idea of technological mind control is not a new one. In *Mind Controllers* author Victorian found evidence of it going back decades. "Dr. Jose Delgado, a neurosurgeon and Yale professor, received funding for brain and electrode research on children and adults. In the 1950's, he developed a miniature electrode that could be placed within an individual's cranium; this electrode was capable of receiving and transmitting electronic signals. Delgado was able to control the movements of his subjects by pushing buttons on a remote transmitter. He demonstrated the potential of his invention by wiring a fully-grown bull. With the device in place, Delgado stepped into the ring with the bull. The animal charged towards the experimenter – and then suddenly stopped, just before it reached him. The powerful beast had been stopped with the simple action of pushing a button on a small box held in Delgado's hand." Since there is evidence of electronic devices being placed in test subjects as far back as the 1950s, imagine how far that has technology has progressed.

The CIA claims that the MKULTRA project was abandoned. I do not think anyone really believes that. It may not be classified under that particular code name, but I feel certain that the CIA or some faction are still actively involved in mind control research and experimentations, most likely on a larger scale than most of us can fathom. Many alien abductees report seeing humans working alongside the aliens. I too have witnessed this. As I previously stated, the humans I have seen were all male and looked like clones of each other. Maybe they were clones, or maybe the extraterrestrials were using the technique of mental or technological camouflage to deceive me into believing that I was seeing humans. They could be a part of some secret black-op team that is indeed working in some capacity with the aliens. The possibilities are numerous as to why black-op factions, of ours or any other government, would be working with an alien presence on Earth. It could be that they are also being controlled by the aliens and have no choice in the matter. Another reason could be the creation of so called "super soldiers."

The humans seen in abduction settings could be using us for completely different purposes than their alien counterparts. New drugs, including vaccinations, could be part of the secret testing as many abductees do come down with unusual and often serious illnesses after an event; some even succumb to it without a cause being known. For some abductees, including me, the opposite is true, and unexplainable good health is the norm. I am convinced that the human workers I have encountered during my experiences were clones. It could be that secret government operatives are there to learn about cloning and transgenic modification process. Two things are clearly evident. They not only know about the alien presence; they are also working with them in some unknown capacity.

Perhaps, our government is helpless to protect us and is forced into cooperating with the aliens. What other choice do they have? In the end, the helpless abductees are the ones suffering the immediate reper-cussions. Not only, are we taken against our will by an alien species, but many of us are also taken by our own species and subjected to more experimentation and interrogation. It is a vicious cycle, a merry-go-round that never stops. In case after case, there is a clear pattern of deception that evolves, and it is used by both the aliens and government operatives. Such is the case with screen memories. Screen memories are often used by the aliens in order to mask the real events of abduction. For example, a person may see some kind of animal such as a deer, monkey, or the commonly used owl. When one of these animals is seen, it may appear out of place. Since the image of the animal is familiar, the person feels no threat. He may discover a period of missing time or may awaken to find unexplainable blood, rashes, puncture marks, or scars. He may be puzzled and alarmed by these physical marks yet have no memory of what happened. If he remembers anything, it will be the screen memory of the out of place but familiar animal.

Many times an abductee, experiencing a screen memory, will not remember the event or question any unusual physical abnormalities stemming from it. Sometimes, however, the real memories of the encounter will begin to surface in vivid dreams or flashbacks. Often the person will seek help from a therapist in order to better understand or validate the memories haunting his everyday life. Under hypnotic regression, more details usually emerge of the actual alien abduction. The trauma from my own experiences first surfaced as a physical symptom. For years the Greys had performed a masterful job of deceiving me and erasing any memories of what they had done to me. Finally, all those abduction experiences that had been locked away in my subconscious reached a tipping point. Mind control no longer worked on me. The trauma surfaced in the form of severe anxiety and panic attacks. I ended up in therapy, and the awakening began. As more and more memories surfaced, I realized the extent of the deception used by the Greys.

The Greys and, most likely, other alien species play on our fears. Through their experiments, they have learned what triggers this basic human instinct. Through implant monitoring, they witness the governments of Earth using fear as an effective tool in deception. They observe various religions using fear to gain followers. They know that fear equals control, and deception is much easier when used in conjunction with fear. The abduction event begins with deception. A small Grey will communicate telepathically with you. He will tell you not to be afraid; they will not hurt you. If they control your fear, either by instigating it or removing it, they are controlling you. They use fear as a means to an end. They know we fear them. They know all the things we fear. As you have read in a previous chapter in this book, countless Experiencers have been shown images of war, nuclear holocaust, catastrophic floods, fires, earthquakes, rampant disease, and famine.

They do this to illicit a fear response in us. Maybe, they are trying to instill a belief in us that they are our benevolent space brothers and are here to save our planet. Those that believe this are easier to control. Once again fear equals control. Their deception is immaculate.

Throughout the UFO community there seems to be a division. There is the "space brothers" camp that believes that the aliens are here to help mankind; they will enlighten us, teach us, heal us, and save our planet. Then there is the other side that believes the aliens have a more sinister plan. Many of them believe that the aliens are here to use us, to take resources from our planet, and possibly take over the Earth. The truth is no one really knows what the agenda for any alien species is. I say this time and time again because, in reality, there are no alien or UFO experts. Everyone is merely guessing or hoping. The entire premise of the alien agenda is subjective and pure conjecture. The abductees/experiencers are the ones who have encountered the extraterrestrials. They have seen their crafts and advanced technology, communicated with them, and even interacted with them sexually. If there are answers to be found, it is with us, the abductees. Most of us do not think our alien puppet masters have our best interest in mind. What they do appears to serve their own agenda and not mankind's.

Evidence suggests that Earth has been visited by extraterrestrials for thousands of years. Over the course of all this time, homo-sapiens have evolved to where we are now. One does not have to be a genius to see that our planet is in dire straits. Pollution, famine, pestilence, constant war, global warming, decline of animal species, water shortages, etc. are the norm at the present time. If any of the aliens visiting and/or inhabiting Earth are here as our cosmic space brothers to save us, then exactly when are they planning on doing it? Where is the evidence? They have certainly had ample time to help and, perhaps, put us on a new and better evolutionary path. Elton Turner made some very valid points in an article he wrote that was published in UFO Universe magazine back in 1993. He wrote, "Before we allow ourselves to believe in the benevolence of the alien interaction, we should ask – do enlightened beings need to use the cover of night to perform good deeds? Do they need to paralyze us and render us helpless to resist? Do "angels" need to steal our fetuses? Do they need to manipulate our children's genitals and probe our rectums? Are fear, pain and deception consistent with high spiritual motives?"

I would like to believe that all advanced species are benevolent. I hold on to the hope that at least some of them are. Of all the aliens that are currently visiting and have visited our planet in the past, I would hope that at least some of them felt compelled to help us in whatever manner they could. It is possible that there are those who do wish to help us, but they are prevented from doing so by a more powerful alien species. As I have previously stated, it is reasonable to believe that a hierarchy exists within the various alien groups interested in our planet and its inhabitants. Just like the various countries on Earth, some are more powerful than others. The less powerful may not like or agree with the actions of more powerful countries, but they are unable to do anything about it and thus are forced to sit idly by and observe the actions and consequences of the more powerful nations. Perhaps, both viewpoints have some truth to them. Realistically, one cannot place all aliens into a simple category. They are not all our space brothers, and they are not all vile, heartless creatures either. The problem is that the more insidious species seem to be in control now, and they do not appear to be leaving any time soon.

This brings me back full circle to my two remaining fears. I have accepted that I cannot do anything to remedy either fear. I am helpless to stop them from taking anyone including a loved one. I also know there is nothing I can do about the implants placed in me or the functions they perform. It matters not if the telepathic powers demonstrated by the Greys are genuine psychic abilities, or if they are simply the result of a highly advanced implant technology. All that matters is that I and others are being monitored and controlled at will by an extraterrestrial race. That fact alone should strike fear in all humanity. How do we know that it is not being done by the aliens on all of us? What better way for them to control the masses than through some sort of nano sized implant? They may not want to rid the planet of humans, only control them. Have they been waiting patiently all this time for our technology to evolve, with their assistance, to the point that this type of undertaking could be done by us and not them? It is an ominous thought. It sounds like a plot in a science fiction movie, but I think one that should be taken into consideration as a part of the possible alien agenda. Obviously, I hope that something like this never happens. However, I do believe that it is within the realm of possibility in the not so distant future should the Greys, and whomever they are working with, desire.

As time passes, the mysteries only deepen in this very complex phenomenon. I have learned much from my decades of interaction with an alien species. I have been privy to things that most humans will never be. I have experienced and witnessed events that many would find incomprehensible. I may have a better understanding about them than most, but even I do not have all the answers, not even close. In the meantime, ufologists will continue their quest for answers, but the truth of the alien agenda remains ever elusive. Perhaps, for now, that is best. Maybe the aliens believe that mankind is not yet prepared for that ultimate truth, or maybe in the end, they will not care if we are ready or not. For me, each day is a new mountain to climb. Each day, I reclaim myself, empower myself, move forward against my detractors, and try to maintain my strength and sanity. The Greys have taken so much from me, but I did not let them win. I know that I am still in here beneath the chaos. Despite it all, my soul is still beautiful. I am stronger than I have ever been, and I will continue to do my best to live a life that is mine.

Chapter 10

CHANGES

"Trauma permanently changes us. This is the big scary truth about trauma: there is no such thing as "getting over it." The five stages of grief model marks universal stages in learning to accept loss, but the reality is in fact much bigger; a major life disruption leaves a new normal in its wake. There is no "back to the old me." You are different now, full stop. This is not a wholly negative thing. Healing from trauma can also mean finding new strength and joy. The goal of healing is not a papering-over of changes in an effort to preserve or present things as normal. It is to acknowledge and wear your new life – warts, wisdom, and all – with courage."

—Catherine Woodiwiss

I love this quote from Catherine Woodiwiss. She perfectly states the ramifications of trauma. You can draw positive aspects from a negative experience by learning to accept and acknowledge what has happened to you. This is not something that will happen overnight. It can take years, but it is imperative for anyone who has gone through the trauma of an alien abduction. I have said many times that you have to learn to empower yourself here in your everyday life. You have no power during abduction, and it can severely impact your self-worth. Even though, many of the experiments and procedures done to abductees are quite heinous; you must not allow yourself to develop a victim mentality from what has been done to you. You will suffer a lot if you do. I spent years feeling sorry for myself; before, I was finally able to pull myself from the depths of despair. I think to some degree all abductees experience this. People, who have never been through these experiences, will never truly understand how profoundly affected we are. The numerous sexual, mental, and physical procedures inflict psychological damage. As if this is not enough, most, who remember, are too afraid to tell anyone about their experiences, so they are left to deal with it on their own. It is no wonder that abductees begin to feel like victims. It is also not surprising that the results of these traumatic experiences eventually manifest.

There are so many abductees experiencing symptoms that a new term (PAS), which stands for Post Abduction Syndrome, has been created for the rapidly emerging syndrome. Post Abduction Syndrome is an anxiety disorder that is closely related to Post Traumatic Stress Disorder. In an article in 2000, Rose Hargrove, RN wrote, "It is characterized by the re-experiencing of abduction related memories, fragments, or distortions of those memories and is accompanied by symptoms of increased anxiety and by avoidance of stimuli related to abduction memories or abduction related events. The affected person may experience levels of anxiety that interfere with functioning in personal, occupational, or social areas. The requisite feature of Post Abduction Syndrome is the development of distinctive symptomatology in relation to the experience of the alien abduction phenomenon which is often ongoing in contrast to Post Traumatic Stress Disorder where the stressor is usually a discrete and time limited occurrence that is not repeated in the individual's lifetime. PAS, in most instances, is the result of the sense or memory of being taken away by force or without consent by extraterrestrial or inter-dimensional entities and the associated physically intrusive or invasive procedures by these alleged entities."

The memories of the abduction events are not erased by the aliens. Instead, they are merely suppressed. They are still ever present in the subconscious mind of the abductee. Whether or not they surface depends on several variables. These variables include how many times the individual was taken, who they were taken by, and what was done to them. I also believe that some of us are allowed to remember, so the memories of certain incidents can be monitored by the aliens. Screen memories are also implemented to ensure that, even if the event is recalled, the abductee will dismiss it as something else. As a result of screen memories, the abductee is left confused; he will often remain quiet due to the uncertainly of what really happened. Sadly, the trauma induced by the alien abduction phenomenon is rarely talked about even though it is usually severe. I have done countless interviews and have been asked some great questions over the years but few relating to the psychological damage resulting from my experiences. I know of three individuals, in 2015 alone, who committed suicide because they could no longer deal with the symptoms that manifested after their abductions. How many more suicides happen for the same reason but are attributed to something else because the person never told anyone about their alien encounters?

Some of the characteristic symptoms of Post Abduction Syndrome are:

- Denial of the event

- Making excuses for the event such as claiming you blacked out or were lost

- Persistent avoidance of stimuli associated with the event

- Adverse emotional reaction to any literature, photos or media depicting alien life forms

- Numbing of emotions, a sort of not feeling anything

- Constant re-experiencing of the abduction event either through flashbacks or lucid dreaming

- Sleep disorders – Not being able to sleep or fear of sleeping, difficulty falling asleep or staying asleep and having an exaggerated startle response when suddenly awakened.

- Anxiety, panic attacks and of course depression

These are just some of the associated symptoms that many of those taken will eventually exhibit. The severity varies from person to person as do the coping abilities of each person. With most abductees, the symptoms of the trauma induced by the abduction experience manifest in other facets of their everyday life. Many become reluctant to enter into relationships. If they are in a relationship or marriage, they may experience guilt if the partner has also been taken. Perhaps, their partner was subjected to sexual procedures, obtrusive gynecological exams, or, worse yet, fetus removal. Sometimes it is difficult for the partner, not being taken, to understand and help the abductee. This causes further isolation and strain on the relationship as many abductees feel alone and helpless. Sometimes substance abuse comes into play as a means to escape, albeit a temporary one. Self-destructive and impulsive behaviors can develop as well.

If you are an abductee, know someone who is, or are living with one, then it is important for you to be aware of these characteristics and symptoms. It is also important for an abductee to know and understand that these symptoms can improve. The one thing that is always constant is change. It will be up to the abductee to decide whether or not that change is positive or negative. I will not sugar coat the process of healing. It is a difficult task. It takes time and should not be done alone. Some kind of support system should be in place. It does not matter whether it is a therapist who is knowledgeable about the subject, a local alien abduction support group, an online support group, or friends and family. You need someone to talk to; you have to gather the courage to talk about what you remember in as much detail as you can. Do not avoid the memories or refrain from certain aspects of them due to possible embarrassment. Those, who truly care about you, will be there for you. Those, who do not accept or believe you, are the ones you do not need anyway.

Never give up! Never, ever give up! There have been times that I felt like giving up, but somehow I have always found the strength to fight and to keep going no matter what. If you have had these experiences, you will eventually realize just how strong you are. That strength will grow as time passes. You have to face your fears; there is no hiding from them. It will be one of the most difficult things you ever do, but, once you do, a dramatic change will begin to take place within you. Your fear will ease or completely subside. You will learn ways to empower yourself. It may take years, but it can be done. I am living proof of it, and I am no different than you or anyone else. Healing from the trauma of alien abductions will not happen overnight. There is no magic spell to make it all go away; that is the reality. Some PAS symptoms will disappear, and others never will. You can learn to live with them and, to some extent, control them instead of them controlling you.

If you are an alien abductee, you do not have to go public with your story like I have done. In fact, I do not recommend it unless you have thick skin and are a really strong person. It is important to talk to someone. There are more people who are willing to listen and believe you, than you realize. That is the first step to recovery. You will be glad you did. Going public is a whole different matter. It can be very rewarding when you know that you have helped others and helped bring about more interest, knowledge and awareness of the subject to the general public. It can also be very frustrating, lonely, and can take an emotional toll on you. People attack what they fear and do not understand. The premise of aliens visiting our planet and taking its inhabitants against their will is too much for many people to comprehend and accept. I think one's religious beliefs play into this as well.

In 2013, I was contacted by a man who said he had been taken numerous times by the Greys. He seemed to be having a difficult time coping with the reality of it. I communicated with him several times. I did my best to answer his questions and offer advice on how to deal with the stress and anxiety he was experiencing. A couple of weeks later, he wrote and said that he had discovered a way to stop his abductions. If I would do it too, my abductions would also cease. He claimed that during a recent abduction experience, he simply called out to Jesus to make them stop. When he did this, the Greys immediately stopped and left his house. He was convinced that they would never return. I thanked him for offering me the information. I told him that I had tried that several times, but it did not stop the aliens from taking me. If it were that simple, there would be no more people being taken; that is certainly not the case. My response made him angry. I never heard from him again, but he made his presence known in another way. He wrote a scathing review of my first book on Amazon. The very same book he said had helped him. In the review, he attacked me personally; he stated I was crazy and should be put in a mental institution. He also said that I was a danger to society. Many people are threatened by the UFO phenomenon and alien abduction, as this does not mesh with their long standing religious convictions.

It is taught by some religions that God made man in his own image. There are some who believe that humans are the superior life form in the universe. Religious beliefs and ego get in the way of the belief in extraterrestrials or ultra-terrestrials. The truth is we are not alone, and we are not even close to being the superior species of the universe. It is a bitter pill to swallow for most, but it is still the truth. For decades, I have been taken by a race of aliens. I have witnessed their mental capabilities. I have seen their technology and what it can do. We are not even close to that level of advancement. Who knows what other alien species are out there that may be even more evolved than the Greys? We can only hope that they are a benevolent species.

Going public as an alien abductee and/or experiencer opens you up to a large number of people who look to you for answers. I do my best to provide answers when I can, and I am honest with others when I do not know the answer. There are those in the UFO field who seem to have a constant need to have their ego stroked and will answer everything regardless of whether it is factual or not. I have seen this many times and find it appalling. Prominent UFO researchers will state what they believe the aliens want or what their agenda is. It is absurd. It reminds me of TV preachers who claim specific knowledge from God, like they have a special phone line to heaven. It is really no different with some in the UFO community who make outlandish claims about aliens. How do they know what the aliens want? How do they know the true agenda of any extraterrestrial species? Do they have direct communication with the aliens and speak with them on a regular basis? Of course not! It is ridiculous. No one is an expert, and no one can say with any certainly what the visitors want or why they want it. It may help to sell tickets at conferences, but it is dishonest. In my humble opinion, it hurts the field. Most of these self-proclaimed UFO experts have never had an actual alien encounter and, yet, claim to know everything about the phenomenon. I have had years of experiences and still cannot say with any certainty what is really happening, except that there is a hybrid program in place. Being realistic and seeing things as they are is a part of the change that has taken place within me over the years. Unfortunately, what I see is usually not very pretty.

There is a disparity between the people who believe in UFOs and aliens and those who do not. The extreme view on both sides can be frustrating. I no longer care if people believe or not. There are some people who will not believe regardless of the evidence in support of UFOs, aliens, and alien abduction; they continue to deny the reality. I have also found the other end of the spectrum. Some believers think that everything is a UFO, or some believe they have been taken because they had a dream one night about an alien. The internet is overrun with videos and photos of alleged UFOs and/or extraterrestrials. There is the infamous "Skinny Bob" video and the alien autopsy one. There is a video of a saucer shaped craft landing in a field; aliens come out and walk around the area by the craft. If you are reading this book, then you, most likely, have seen these videos or others like them. One of the more recent changes I have made is that I have stopped examining UFO videos and photos for people. In the past, I would often get UFO videos or photos, but people would get angry with me if I debunked the video or photo by explaining what it really was. They wanted to believe so badly that they would not accept the truth.

I distinctly remember the case of a woman from Florida who sent me two photos that she had taken. She claimed that one of them was a UFO hovering over her house, and the other photo was of a small Grey hiding in the bushes in her backyard. I am no photo analysis expert, nor do I claim to be. Those skills, however, were not necessary when it came to the photos she sent. I uploaded the first photo and zoomed in on the object she thought was a UFO. It was obvious what the object really was; it was a bird's nest. There was a light pole beside the tree, and it was easy to see that branches were holding up the nest. Needless to say, after that, I was not overly thrilled to look at the other photo, which was supposed to be of an alien. I was highly skeptical of this even before I saw it. I do not believe that any alien would allow itself to be photographed. Either through heat sensors or their own mental prowess, they know what other life forms are near. They would know if anyone attempted to photograph or film them, and they would confiscate it. They do not go to such great lengths to hide themselves from our world to allow someone to easily photograph them.

When I examined the second photo, it turned out to be exactly what I had thought it was going to be, a classic case of pareidolia. This is the phenomenon of seeing a familiar shape or form in random combinations of shadows and light when none exist. This happens most often with people believing they have caught a ghost on film but can also apply to other supernatural creatures such as Bigfoot, aliens, etc. I do believe that ghosts and Bigfoot creatures have been photographed; there is legitimate evidence out there. However, I have never seen a convincing picture or video of an actual alien. As I observed the photo of the alleged alien in the bushes, I saw nothing. Finally after several minutes, I could make out the shape of the typical Grey's head with the big eyes, but it was clearly not an alien. It was apparent to me that this woman deeply wanted to see and film a UFO over her house. Because of this desire, her mind created a bird's nest into a UFO and shadows and light into an alien. When I contacted her with my conclusions, she got angry. I did my best to explain to her, in the nicest way possible, what I had found and how I had come to my conclusion, but it was to no avail. She had made up her mind before she sent me the photos; she was looking for further validation. When she did not get it, she lashed out at me. Such is life for an abductee who goes public.

As I have gotten older, my perspective of the UFO phenomenon has changed. Instead of answers, I have gotten more questions. The more I learn; the less I realize I know, for it is a very complex field. I do feel, however, that I have learned many truths during this long journey. I have spoken publicly about most of them. Several insights that I have shared were a bit controversial, but I have noticed that other researchers are now agreeing and speaking about some of the same things. I hope that my contributions to the alien abduction field have helped it to progress. I hope that my story has helped bring about more awareness to the subject and helped convince people that we are not all delusional or experiencing sleep paralysis; we are normal people from all walks of life. Most of all, I hope that others who have endured these terrifying events have found solace and inspiration in my story. If so, then this has all been worth it.

I have raised a few eyebrows within the UFO community because of my support of the US government and for support of nondisclosure. I simply believe that society is not ready, and disclosure would result in utter chaos. Does anyone seriously believe that the United States government is suddenly going to admit they have been lying to us for decades; admit they have known about abduction; admit they have worked alongside the aliens during these events; admit they have covered them up for a trade off of alien technology? They would also have to admit that ours or any other countries' industrial military complex is totally helpless in stopping the extraterrestrials and protecting the citizens of Earth.

Full disclosure of any alien presence will happen when, and if, an alien race decides. Yet, soft disclosure is happening all the time. It is slowly being leaked into the fabric of our society in sometimes subtle and sometimes obvious ways. Humans are being acclimated to the idea that we are not alone in the universe. Mainstream media and NASA play an important role in this. Scientists and astronomers are frequently making announcements about new planets being discovered that could support life. Some have gone so far as to say earth like planets have been discovered. I have seen articles supporting the premise of using worm holes for space travel; I have witnessed and stated this for years. The aliens are using dimensional portals for travel and to abduct humans. Even Pope Francis has begun to speak of aliens. As time goes on, these kinds of things will help to soften the blow, so to speak, when, and if, the visitors ever reveal themselves to us.

Even though I have publicly stated my support for the government's nondisclosure, they still monitor me. I do not blame them; I would monitor someone like me too. In 2014, I was paid a personal visit by two gentlemen, who I believe were representatives from the "secret government." It happened one day while I was visiting a small town about thirty minutes east of Las Vegas called Boulder City. It is a charming place which garners its share of tourists due to its proximity to Hoover Dam. The historic downtown area is full of cool little shops and eateries. One such shop, Area 52, has an alien theme and is full of all kinds of alien oriented merchandise and books. It had been several years since I had been there, so, on that particular day, I decided to drop in and take a look around.

The store was not very busy when I first entered; there were only two customers who left shortly after I arrived. I shopped for several minutes and then decided to leave. There were a couple of book shelves placed near the front door. I stopped to look through a few books on the way out. Then I noticed a man who came in alone. He was well dressed in a nice dark colored suit. I thought that his attire was a bit peculiar for a tourist section of town where almost everyone was casually dressed. I kept glancing up from the book I was thumbing through to look at him. He walked around the store quickly looking around in all directions as if he was casing the place. Shortly thereafter, he walked straight to the cash register. The impeccably dressed man leaned over the counter and spoke with the cashier. Immediately, she exited through a door that was directly behind the cash wrap counter. He then walked past me and left the store, without acknowledging my presence. I thought his behavior was rather odd since he seemed to be scouting the store instead of shopping. I also could not figure out what his conversation with the cashier was about since she still had not returned from the back room. I remained at the end of the book display by the front door entrance.

Less than a minute later, the man in the suit returned followed by a much older gentleman. The older man was dressed casually in jeans and a short sleeved shirt. The man in the suit walked to the back of the store and positioned himself where he could see both the front door and the cash wrap. The older guy appeared to be in his 80's. He did not continue into the store but stopped about a foot away from me. He wasted no time in striking up a conversation. Without hesitation, he asked me if I believed in UFOs; I answered that I did. He then rather bluntly asked me if I had ever seen one. This question made me chuckle a bit; I answered that I had indeed seen one. He smiled as he realized he had "broken the ice" so to speak.

I was not prepared for what the next several minutes was about to deliver. He told me that he knew who I was. That statement, in and of itself, did not surprise me. After all, my picture was on the book, and I had done quite a lot of media. I figured he recognized me from either place, so I asked him if he had read my book. He said that he was aware of it but did not directly answer whether or not he had read it. Given the unusual circumstances of the entire situation, I started to feel apprehensive and thought about excusing myself and leaving, but my curiosity about the mysterious older gentleman and his well-dressed partner got the best of me. I decided to continue with the intriguing conversation. After all, he seemed harmless, and he had a pleasant personality. I was a little surprised when he suddenly asked me if I knew who he was. It seemed to him that I should know him, but I did not remember ever meeting him. He then began to tell me his story.

He had begun his career in the Navy. Sometime during his early years in the Navy, he was chosen to work in special secret programs. I asked him why he was chosen. He said that it was because of his training in electronics combined with his ability to follow orders and keep quiet. He laughed as he said it, and so did I. I was suspicious as to why he was revealing this information to me. I knew there was more to this than just a casual conversation. I began to understand who these two gentlemen were; I still did not know why they were talking to me. I asked him what kind of secret programs he had worked on, not really expecting to get an answer. To my surprise, he told me that it involved back engineering of advanced technology from alien space craft. Needless to say, his reply garnered my full attention. He continued to tell me how top German scientists were brought over to the United States after World War II. Some of them were involved in the project. He also stated that they had "other help." I asked him who else helped in these projects. He simply stated, "Aliens." I followed up, "What kind of aliens?" There was a mannequin of a Tall Grey in a corner close to where we were standing; he pointed to it and said, "They looked like that guy."

At this point, I did not know what to say. One thing was certain; I knew he was not joking. He must have noticed the perplexed look on my face as he continued talking. He explained that the Tall Greys worked with us on all kinds of technology. They had helped us with the invention of our new devices. He briefly mentioned the size of some of the research facilities; some were underground while others were hidden in plain sight. He spoke about bending gravity, worm holes, and dimensional portals. He mentioned a few scientific terms which I did not understand. I was completely blown away by what I was hearing. For some reason, I felt compelled to ask him what he knew about the Philadelphia Experiment (the teleportation and time travel experiment allegedly carried out by the U.S. Navy in 1943). I was told by the old gentleman that it did indeed happen, but not in the way it had been depicted in movies and books. He added that those kinds of experiments are still being conducted and have gotten much more refined. I had to know why he was telling me all of this, so I asked him. Although retired, he still had ties to that part of the government. He nodded towards the well dressed man standing by the back wall and said that he still worked for the programs. He explained that they knew who I was, and he was asked to approach me because of his age and personality. He said they knew that I understood the complexity of the subject matter. I was helping them, in a sense, by telling my story and putting out the information that I have. They wanted me to know that I am "100% correct," and I was told to keep up the good work.

The well-dressed man approached us and said, "Time to go" to the older man. I shook the older man's hand and mustered up a meager "thank you." They quickly exited the store. I stood there for a few minutes trying to process the chain of events that had just happened. The clerk had still not returned; I felt an eerie silence fill the store. I realized that I had just been contacted by an agent and former agent of the secret black op government. It all felt surreal. I placed the book, I had been holding, back on the shelf and left. As I walked down the sidewalk to my car, I heard the beep of a horn. The sound came from a large passenger van with windows. Next to the driver was the man wearing the suit. The older gentleman was sitting directly behind the driver; he smiled and waved as they passed. I nodded my head and waved back. For some reason, this strange meeting reinvigorated me. I had a strong visceral feeling that I was on the right track and doing what I was supposed to do.

There is no denying that these obtrusive events have had a profound effect on my life. I have only gotten glimpses of a "normal" life. I have lived a double life and still do. At times, I have to keep my dark secret hidden; I pretend to be a regular person living a normal life. I wish it did not have to be like this, but, unfortunately, our society has not yet reached that level of belief and acceptance. Fear is still prevalent. It is my hope that my books and media appearances will in some small way help bring about more acceptance and awareness. Maybe one day, Experiencers will not have to endure what we do today.

Living life as an alien abductee is very difficult. I do not think anyone can fully understand what it is like unless he/she has experienced it as well. You live each day knowing that, at any given moment, you could be taken again. I used to dread going to sleep because so many events had happened while sleeping; I often wished that humans did not require sleep. I have lived a life of loneliness and have always felt different. Keeping your experiences secret only adds to the feelings of isolation and loneliness. It is not easy to live with the truth of the alien reality. A major portion of the population still does not believe; they are completely unaware of what is really happening here on Earth. I have suffered nosebleeds, cuts, scratches, rashes and scars from alien procedures. I have endured bouts of deep depression and severe anxiety which eventually led to therapy. These are the physical and mental consequences of being taken by beings that most people do not believe even exist. I have been examined by doctors who offer no explanation for the scars on my body or the recurring nose bleeds. I have submitted to a QEEG brain scan to prove I was not delusional. In fact, the results showed no brain tumors, a high intellect, and a superior memory. I have passed a polygraph test; I have provided photographic evidence. I have shared an abduction experience with someone who publicly validated everything that happened to us. I have presented cases in this book with similarities to my case that defy the odds. I have done all I can do to prove the reality of the alien abduction phenomenon. At the very least, I hope I have opened some minds to the possibility.

For many years I was angry about what happened to me. I was angry at my alien captors; I was angry that it happened at all. I felt sorry for myself. I never asked to be taken; I certainly never wanted it. I often asked myself the big question of pity. Why me? I resented them for taking me. I resented having to keep it a secret for all those years. I hated living with the reality of it. I was envious of everyone else who lived normal lives. I tried my best to fit in and still do, but it is always there lurking in the shadows of my mind. I used to think that my awakening took place with the breakthrough revelations about my alien abductions. I was wrong. The real awakening has taken place in the last few years. It was only when I quit resisting and accepted my fate that I truly began to heal. I know and accept that I cannot stop them from taking me. I know that I cannot prevent them from taking my loved ones, should they choose to do so. I have quit feeling sorry for myself. I am no longer angry. I have learned that you cannot choose your experiences, but you can choose your reality. I have refused to become a victim.

I am now at a point in life where my perspective about my experiences has changed. I now focus on the positive aspects of what has happened to me. Some may wonder how any of these horrific incidents could result in anything positive in one's life. There are actually numerous positives that are a result of my life of alien abductions. I started practicing meditation to overcome the anxiety and depression that I was experiencing due to these encounters. Meditation was instrumental in the healing process for me. In fact, it helped me more than anything. I still meditate on a regular basis; it has changed my life for the better. If I had never been taken, I might not have discovered the profound value in practicing meditation. Also, I have always had excellent health. I am sure that the Greys have had something to do with this. It may have been to their benefit to keep me healthy, but I also benefitted. I used to take my health for granted, but that has changed as I have aged. I have become much more aware of just how fortunate I am to have had such good health. I am altruistic. I am an advocate for the disadvantaged, the environment, animal welfare, and human rights. Because of my experiences, I see things in a different way; they made me love and appreciate mother Earth and her inhabitants. They made me want to help and change things for the better. My interest in organized dogmatic religion waned and was replaced by an increase in spirituality.

The dimensional portals have left me and many other Experiencers with increased psychic abilities by increasing our natural chi and our vibration rate. I have learned to embrace these psychic abilities, especially those relating to spirit communication. I have used them to help many people both in this plane of existence and in the realm of the spirits. From the time I was 12 years old, I recognized an ability to use energy to help heal others. I later learned Reiki but realized I was already naturally doing it. My chi is powerful; it is that way because of what has happened to me. Had I not had these experiences, I, most likely, would not have the energy I do or have the ability to read and feel energy; I would not be able to help others with it. Also, my experiences have caused a decrease in materialism which I have found to be a very positive thing. I have met many wonderful people because of my abductions, and I have talked to some of the most fascinating people and have developed strong friendships with many of them. Because of my experiences and going public with my story, I have met one of the most beautiful souls I have ever known; she has been a true godsend in my life.

Yes, there are many positive things that I have discovered because of my experiences. I did not let the Greys ruin my life; I used what they did to me to make me a better person. They made me strong. One does not live through what I have without becoming stronger. They made me see things in ways I never would have; they revealed truths to me that many will never know. They made me take a long hard look at myself and strive to make myself a better human being. They made me value kindness, love, and compassion, and I have seen how sorely lacking it is in our world. They made me dismiss ego and understand that our species is not the supreme beings of the universe. They made me appreciate our wondrous planet. I no longer blame the Greys for what they did; they are doing it because they have to, just as we would if the circumstances dictated. I no longer wish that this had never happened to me. In fact, the opposite is true. It has all been instrumental in making me who I am, and I am proud of the man I have become. It has been a long, arduous journey, but along the way, I have learned so much. I am finally at peace. It has taken decades, but I can finally say this to the Greys. I forgive you...

Works Cited List :

http://www.conciseencyclopedia.com/

www.biblehub.com

www.ropercenter.cornell.edu

www.usatoday.com

Lorgen, Eve, MA. Alien Love Bite. USA: Elogos & HHC Press, (Feb. 14, 2000)

www.merriam-webster.com

http://www.annunaki.org/

Hargrove RN, Rose. "Post Abduction Syndrome (PAS): Description of an Emerging Syndrome" (HTML). Paper. (Feb. 14, 2000)

Tellinger, Michael. African Temples of the Anunnaki: The Lost Technologies of the Gold Mines of Enki. Bear & Company (May 24, 2013)

www.sitchin.com

Valle, Jacques. Passport To Magonia: On Ufo's, Folklore, and Parallel Worlds. Contemporary Books; Softcover edition, (May, 1993)

Jacobs, David M. Secret Life: Firsthand, Documented Accounts of UFO Abductions. USA: Simon and Schuster, (April 16, 1993)

Oldham, Bret. Children of the Greys. USA: House of Halo, (April, 2013)

www.psychicpulse.com

Stenger, Victor J. Bioenergetic Fields. The Scientific Review of Alternative Medicine, Vol. 3, No. 1, (Spring/Summer, 1999)

Turner, Elton. UFO Universe, Vol.3 No.1. Kelt Works Inc. (Spring 1993)

Victorian Dr, Armen, Dr. Mind Controllers. VISION Paperbacks (April 1999)

Made in the USA
Columbia, SC
17 February 2023

12267603R00087